THIS ONE THING I DO

The Story of Alice Weed

Dr. Evelyn Miller Berger

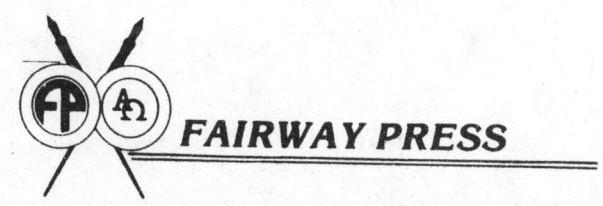

FAIRWAY PRESS

THIS ONE THING I DO

FIRST EDITION
Copyright © 1983 by
Fairway Press
Lima, Ohio

All rights reserved. No portion of this book may be reproduced or utilized in any form or by any means, electronic or mechanical including photocopying, without permission in writing from the publisher. Inquiries should be addressed to: Fairway Press, 628 South Main Street, Lima, Ohio 45804.

Second Printing 1986
Third Printing 1987

7508/ISBN 0-89536-957-5   PRINTED IN U.S.A. BY FAIRWAY PRESS

CONTENTS

Preface v
1. A Single Purpose 1
2. The Door Opens 9
3. On the Way 20
4. China at Last 26
5. Language School and War 40
6. Land of Diversity 49
7. Kien Yang Beginnings 60
8. Making Do 70
9. Travel in Szechwan 82
10. India 90
11. Return to Kien Yang 98
12. Arrival of the Communists 112
13. Under Communist Rule 122
14. No Way Out? 138
15. Permission to Leave 146
16. A Different Land, a Different Opportunity ... 154
17. Costa Rica 163
18. Endless Line of Splendor 172
19. China Thirty-two Years Later 177

PREFACE

We were visiting Costa Rica where my father, Bishop George A. Miller, had established Methodist work in 1916. In church women's groups, in Sunday schools, in many of the eighty-three preaching places as well as on the Mission Farm in San Carlos, I heard about Alice Weed.

It was "Mees Weed did this," "Mees Weed went there," or "Mees Weed said thus and so."

The owner of the name soon returned from furlough in the States. Charming, efficient, and full of fun, she was soon busy with her crowded schedule of extensive work in the beautiful little country of Costa Rica.

Someone's chance remark indicated that she had been a refugee from China when the Communists had taken over the country. When I asked her about it, the answers to my questions were startling.

Current books, magazine articles, and tourist reports give a far different picture from the China of the 1940s. Earlier publications, letters to her family kept and filed, and my own recollections of China which I had seen in childhood have furnished helpful details in weaving together this significant story.

In no sense is this a chronicle of China's political and military struggles in the 1940s. It was a tumultuous time of rapid emergence of an enormous, unwieldy mass of people into an amazingly orderly nation. But as she pulled herself together, China roughly, at times cruelly, rejected all that was foreign.

Nor is this a page of missionary history in China. It is the story of a dedicated life, a life with one purpose and one only: Sharing the Christian message with people in a foreign land. Blocked repeatedly, Alice Weed held to her goal in spite of seemingly insurmountable obstacles.

Space limitations, unhappily, dictate the omission of many important names and places. The following pages record some of the events in a remarkable life which, it is hoped, will give the delight and inspiration to others that it has given to me.

Evelyn Miller Berger

1
A Single Purpose

The little summer resort of Rye perched comfortably at the foot of Colorado's Mount Baldy. The fickle stream beside the town was a well-behaved little creek most of the year. But after the snow blanketing the lofty Rockies melted, the stream became a raging torrent.

People usually covered the thirty-two miles from the town of Pueblo by horse and buggy. Automobiles had not yet learned to climb steep grades. Later the mailman's Model-T Ford was the first to make the attempt, but even that amazing vehicle had to back the last three miles into town. The gravity fuel feed had difficulty reaching the engine of the straining, puffing little automobile.

It was the twenty-fifth of May. Spring was bursting out across the countryside. When the Pueblo doctor was summoned to a Rye emergency, his horse and buggy made the trip in record time.

A cloud of tragedy hung over Joe Weed's two-story, white frame house in Rye. In the upstairs bedroom, the doctor looked up from the quiet figure on the bed. He shook his head. His best medical skills had failed to staunch the childbirth hemorrhage. The life of the young mother was slowly ebbing away.

No one was giving attention to the pitiful bit of

humanity left for dead in a pan in the corner. Then, the midwife glanced back into the shadows beyond the reach of the flickering coal oil lamp. Suddenly she exclaimed, "The baby's alive! I saw her move."

She began hot and cold baths to try to revive the tiny spark of life. How little she knew of the dramatic future of the life she was saving!

The white face on the pillow broke into a radiant smile. She had brought a new life into the world. Her eyes looked up into the face of her devoted husband.

The baby's right shoulder had been dislocated in the difficult breech birth; but, without x-rays, the doctor thought it had been broken. He set it in a rigid cast held to the baby's side. The shoulder damage was to cause a disfigured, useless arm.

Time slipped away in the shadowed upstairs bedroom. Three hours went by and the eyes of the young mother slowly glazed, then closed, never to open again.

The town grieved with tall, thin Joe Weed. Friends came to express sympathy. As Joe held his newborn daughter in his arms, the midwife who had saved her life asked, "What will you call her?"

"She's such a wee thing," he murmured tenderly. His eyes filled with tears. "Blanche had chosen the name Alice Lucile. That and life were all her mother could give her." Looking down, "Your mother is gone," he told his baby daughter. "You're left to comfort me. You are my little Alice in Wonderland." And that was what he called her, even writing a poem later with that fairy tale name.

Fresh shocks of grief struck Joe Weed again and again. Personal belongings, even furniture and dishes in their simple home, gave reminders of his overwhelming loss. Friends and neighbors had their own lives to lead, and their visits lessened.

Quiet, soft-spoken Joe Weed was hard-working

and dependable. His deep, blue eyes looked out on life with a serene confidence that God was in His heaven, so all must be right with the world. His unmarried sister, Kate, plump, good-natured "Aunt Tee," had come to Rye to help with the new baby. Now she remained to mother little Alice, manage Joe's household and help with his farm and job as postmaster. Her twinkling eyes and unfailing common sense saved many unnecessarily tense situations.

When Alice's Christian Science grandmother came to visit, she told Alice that her arm was all right and it should be used normally. Alice prayed that it might be so and made every effort to follow her grandmother's advice. She carried her school books with her deformed arm, hoping to straighten it. She tried to hang from the hayloft rafters to pull it into normal position. But nothing helped.

Alice's father and her Aunt Tee never suggested that she might be different from other children. She was to expect no special consideration. There was no opportunity to withdraw in self-pity, and she learned to take care of herself with cheerful good humor. She grew up believing that she could do what any other little girl could do.

But trouble seemed to stalk her life. When she was barely four years old, a severe siege of typhoid fever threatened her life. Only her unusual vitality carried her through. She finally regained her strength, and again became a healthy, happy-go-lucky little girl. But her right arm, set in an unnatural position, was painful. Any chance jolt caused excruciating distress.

With typical childhood insensitivity, other children made fun of the crippled arm. Alice tried to play baseball and basketball; but since she could only throw and catch with one arm, she was seldom chosen for a playground team.

She heartily disliked arithmetic. Her father told

her how to find answers to problems, but he insisted that she work them out herself. Later in high school, she would have gone down to defeat in geometry if he had not again come to her rescue.

"Geometry," he told her, "is like life. You must take it a step at a time."

"I was impulsive," Alice said in later years. "I was always in a hurry to skip over details and leap to a conclusion. Like so many lessons from my father, I learned to follow steady, logical guidelines and avoid ill-advised, hasty missteps."

There was much to learn about life. A lively curiosity invited adventure. She disobeyed the rules when she slipped off one time to play with a newborn calf in the corral. When the enraged cow turned to chase her over the fence, her father arrived with a waving pitchfork just in time to avoid disaster. When future ill-advised interests tempted her to break other rules, Alice remembered the hot breath of an angry cow at her heels.

One day when her aunt left on an errand, she told Alice not to leave the house while she was away. But Alice took off to play at a neighbor's. She was not "caught," but her guilty conscience made her miserable. It became a more forceful guide than any fear of punishment. The budding respect for truth was only one of the many lessons learned from a loving father and aunt.

Alice and her father were constant companions. Sometimes he swung Alice up to his broad shoulders, and she was convinced that at six foot three, he was the tallest man in the world. On Sunday mornings before church, they often went out to check the farm crops, and Joe explained how God made the plants grow, the mountains reach to the sky, and the birds sing. God, she learned, was as near as the buzzing bees, the warm sunshine, and the soft breeze touching her cheek.

When World War I broke out, Joe was beyond enlistment age; but his younger brother, Fred, entered the service. Joe moved his little family to Kansas to take over his brother's farm. Alice was eight years old. She had never known brothers and sisters, and enjoyed the happy family with several cousins. She also had the experience of adjusting to a large household, living intimately with the confusion of many people coming and going. She did not know that it was good preparation for later, more difficult, experiences living with large groups of busy people.

One Sunday morning, Alice and her father looked across the beautiful crop of wheat. It was taller than Alice.

"It's ready for the header," Joe observed.

"Then aren't you going to skip church to harvest it?" Alice wondered.

"No," answered her father. "This is the Lord's Day. We're going to church to worship as usual."

A Kansas hail storm came up during the service. By late afternoon the wheat lay flat on the ground, and the next day it had to be cut out with the mower. Most of the grain was lost.

Children at school taunted Alice.

"Your father's a religious crank," they jeered. "See? Your crop's ruined!"

Alice went home crestfallen. Her father was unperturbed.

"The Lord knows what we need," he said comfortably. "He will provide."

It was another guideline for times of dire difficulty in Alice's future years. She decided she would do what seemed to be right at the time, and have faith that the future would bring solutions as needed.

When the war was over, Fred returned from his service in the Army. He took over his home responsibilities, and Joe moved Alice and Aunt Tee to a rented farm. They enjoyed no luxuries. Every Saturday they took milk and eggs to town to trade for flour, sugar, and other essentials. A tenth of all they had was set aside for the church. If anything was left over, Alice might be given five cents for spending. On rare occasions, she reveled in the delights of an incredibly delicious ice cream cone.

Leaving Aunt Tee and Alice on the rented farm, Joe Weed spent several months of advanced study in Chicago. He trained to be a lay minister, and later served effectively in that capacity.

When Alice was a high school sophomore, a missionary spoke at church one day. She talked of the need for workers in the Punjab of India. Alice was so stirred that she decided she would dedicate her life to try to meet those needs.

When she told her father about her decision, he laughed.

"Oh, you've talked about going into so many different occupations," he said. "This is just another on the list."

"No, no!" Alice exclaimed. "This is different. I feel a deep urge, a real 'call.'"

When her father realized that Alice was in earnest, he told her that her mother had always wanted to be a missionary.

She read everything she could find about India. Her resolve to spend her life working in foreign lands began to take shape. It steadily grew stronger.

Her aunt was understanding. On warm nights, they often slept out in the yard under the stars. One night, looking up into the brilliant heavens overhead, Alice said, "Those stars shine down on people in other countries, too, don't they? They seem to beckon me. Like the Star of Bethlehem, they point the way. So many people around the world have things like cattle, mangers, and straw. But they have no Christ Child to bring them the peace and love that only God can give."

Her lively spirit of adventure persisted, prompting an occasional adolescent resistance to rules. When a warm spring day stirred restless, youthful energies, it was Alice who led the entire school to walk out at the close of the morning assembly. They had no organized plan for the day, but wandered about in carefree irresponsibility. Luckily, when they went home at dinnertime, understanding adults merely laughed and suggested they stay at school the next day.

Then, one day, when she was a senior in high school, her father came to her with a startling question. "You will soon be leaving for college and your own life. I'll be lonely. Would you approve if I married again? There is a longtime friend, a widow, and..."

Alice looked with warm affection at the father who had been the center of her life.

"Of course," she answered. "I have always dreamed I would have somebody someday I could call 'Mother.'"

But immediately after the wedding, Alice's new stepmother came to her.

"There's not room here for both of us," she said tartly. Alice gasped. "This is my farm," continued the stepmother. "Your father is coming to live with me here. That does not include you."

Alice had heard the story of Cinderella's jealous stepmother, but she had never expected to meet her in real life.

The stepsister and two stepbrothers accepted Alice, but their mother flatly declared that Alice was "not to step foot on my place in the future."

Alice was soon to be in college, unable to go home to see her father. He faced a choice between his wife and his daughter. He considered divorce but decided to try to build a good marriage with the woman to whom he had pledged fidelity for better or for worse. The only time Alice ever saw her father genuinely angry was an occasion when her stepmother treated her with unusual unkindness. His marriage was to last for forty turbulent years.

Alice had to arrange to meet him in a different town years later when she bid him good-bye as she left for a foreign country.

2
The Door Opens

When Alice registered at the University of Nebraska, she had to earn her way. She was fortunate to find work for room and board in the home of a kind and friendly family.

On Thanksgiving Day, in her freshman year, her hostess put the turkey in the oven and the whole family left to attend a football game. Alice remained to watch the oven. She became so engrossed in the game on radio, she forgot about the turkey. When the family returned, hungry and ready for a Thanksgiving feast, the turkey was burned black. The hostess said nothing, trimmed off the blackened outside and served what was left without comment. Alice never forgot the lesson in responsibility or the kindness of the family. She remained with them until her junior year.

Typing and other odd jobs provided funds for expenses other than room and board. In her senior year, she was able to live with relatives where she continued to make her way helping with the housework.

She registered for university courses which offered the best preparation for her chosen life's work. Her long working hours to earn her expenses limited her social life; but she was able to join a group of students called Student Volunteers. They were all planning to devote their lives to missionary work in foreign countries.

A young man in one of her classes startled her one day when he asked her for a date. She hesitated, then accepted.

The evening brought another lesson. Her smooth-talking escort spent most of the time telling her how lovely she was. She was bored and irritated. She had never been concerned with beauty and popularity. She tried to interest the light-hearted young man in her ambition to be a missionary. He looked at her with a blank stare, and they parted with no mention of another date. Her goal of Christian service in another country far outweighed any interest in another date.

Because of her life dedication and disregard of her crippled arm, friends hesitated to point out that no mission board would accept a candidate with such a physical handicap. They suggested that she find work among American Indians.

"There are just as many heathen here in the United States as anywhere else," they told her. "They need you, too."

Alice listened with uncertainty. This was not her goal.

However, after graduating from the university with an elementary teaching credential, she took and passed the civil service examination and accepted a position among the Navajo Indians in New Mexico. The teaching experience, she believed, would provide further preparation for work as a missionary. Her original goal remained unchanged.

Her experiences on the Indian reservation provided new insights into human relationships. Police went about each morning on horseback rounding up children for school. Many pupils had to be given names and taught to speak English.

The government did not recognize the Indian marriage ceremony. Each couple had to be married by a civil or religious service. One day, the parents of some of her school children came to the mission to be married. The bride was hostile. When it came time for her to say the customary "yes," she refused to answer. No coaxing, begging, or demanding moved her. Everyone sat down and waited. After some time she burst out with an angry "Yes!"

During all of this time, the bride's mother had been hiding in a coat closet in the hall. If she looked at her son-in-law, the Indians believed, either bride or groom or both would become blind.

Alice had heartily disliked memorizing poetry in grade school, but a sensitivity to beauty always hovered close at hand. In New Mexico, she was awed by the wonder of the desert. Sitting quietly, "You hear its message," she said. "Even the bugs crawling in the sand make a sound. The voices of people too far away to be seen can be heard." She came to love the desert and the Navajo people.

It was a year of intensive "teacher training." She enjoyed her work, but it was not leading to the fulfillment of her purpose to work in a foreign country.

She had saved from her meager salary, but it was not sufficient for the study she hoped to pursue at the Kennedy School of Missions in Hartford, Connecticut.

She had no money to get there, but one day she saw an advertisement in the newspaper. Two women who were driving east wanted a "traveling companion." Alice was not sure what "traveling companion" might mean; but she answered the ad, was accepted, and set forth without knowing that both women suffered severe vision handicaps. They were unable to read road signs and often failed to see oncoming traffic. It was a harrowing journey, but she arrived intact and commented wryly, "I guess the Lord must want me to stay around for a while."

After arriving in Boston, Alice looked for a job to earn money for her tuition. She boarded a train and soon discovered that it ducked underground, and she got off to find herself in a subway. She had no idea how to get out and turned to a little man sitting in something like a cage selling tickets. He told her to take the escalator. She had never heard of an escalator and waited for the arrival of the next train to watch what the disembarking passengers would do. Then her courage failed as she contemplated stepping onto that terrifying, moving stairway. At last, she mustered her last ounce of courage and reached the welcome sunshine on the street above.

Eventually, she found a job in a little neighborhood store. It provided for room and board, and supported her until the seminary opened. Long afterward, the seminary dormitory matron told her that on Alice's arrival she had questioned whether it could ever be possible to "tame this country rustic with the speech of a wild westerner."

During her second year in Hartford, Alice met a Dr. Sweet, who told her that surgery might correct the problem with her arm; but it had never been tried with a person her age. She was now twenty-four. For the first time, she faced the reality of her handicap. She had been so convinced of her "call" to be a missionary, she had ignored the truth of her disability. Now she saw the high hurdle blocking her way. No mission board would accept a candidate with a useless arm. Although past efforts to find medical help had failed, the doctor said that surgery in early childhood could have been entirely successful.

The doctor warned of inevitable pain. Healing would demand patience. He asked if Alice was willing to face it. He would give his medical skills as a contribution to the cause of missions. Alice had to borrow money for hospital expenses, although the Women's Board of the Seminary was willing to provide some financial assistance. She was able later to repay the loan from her monthly salary of fifty dollars while she was teaching on the Sioux Indian Reservation during the next few years.

For several months after the surgery, her arm was supported by a brace held at right angles to her shoulder. She looked as though she were waving. People on the street waved back. Since it was winter, the brace under her coat was not in sight. Even the police would stop traffic to let her cross the street. The professors would look up in class and ask, "Yes, Miss Weed?" After the brace was removed, they would look about and ask, "Where is Miss Weed?"

But the operation was a success. The arm regained fifty percent more use; and it was a gala day when, for the first time in her life, she held a tea cup in her hand and drank from it. She showed unusual manual dexterity. She could "fix anything." She was the daughter of a skilled father who had built his own house in Colorado.

A group of eighteen students at the seminary made plans for an ecumenical project in Tibet where there had been no mission work. They represented various denominations: Quakers, Mennonites, Presbyterians, Episcopalians, Congregationalists, and Methodists. Alice had been baptized in the little Methodist church in Rye; but later in Athol, Kansas, there had been no Methodist church so she had gone to the Congregational church where her father served several years as the lay pastor. She was quite comfortable with the concept of ecumenism.

The students of "The Gang," as they nicknamed themselves, applied to their various denominational boards, but eventually these bodies decided that they were not ready to undertake such an ecumenical venture. The students decided that they would go individually, seeking stations as near as possible to their field of Tibet. Alice's interest began to focus on western China.

After two years of study at the Kennedy School of Missions, Alice received the degree of Master of Arts in Education. The following summer she went to South Dakota to help conduct a Vacation Bible School as a project of the Friend's Service Committee. It was sponsored by the Episcopalian Mission, Methodists, and Roman Catholics. She was to use the Government Day School on the Rosebud Sioux Indian Reservation. That summer, temperatures rose to one hundred eighteen degrees. No trees offered shade for playing. Nevertheless, the Catholic Sisters in their black flowing robes took their part in the baseball games and the vacation school proved to be an experience in ecumenism.

That fall, Alice accepted a teaching position in a public school for white children on the reservation. The salary was far below that offered by the civil service on the Navajo Reservation. However, it gave her the opportunity for more involvement in the Episcopal mission. Alice remarked a number of times that life is full of surprises which are so wonderful that they far outweigh the hardships. She remained three years teaching in the rural schools.

In 1936, the dust bowl devastated the countryside. The Indians were given cattle branded "ERA" to replace cattle that died of hunger and thirst. They dubbed them "Eat-right-away cows" because they were to be eaten rather than used to rebuild the herds that had been lost. The farmers toiled to wrest a living from the parched soil, and it was not unusual during the winter to wake up in the morning to discover the snow covered with red soil that had blown north from

Oklahoma during the night. In the summer, the grasshoppers ate the clothes off the clotheslines and found their way into the houses where they hopped over the dining table. They ate every green plant, even the leaves on the trees.

That winter Alice lived with a young couple in a sod house and walked to school over trackless prairie. The children sometimes came on horseback and sometimes on foot. Finally, the first week of January brought one of the worst storms in history. School had to be closed because of the danger of the children losing their way to and from school. It didn't open again until the first of March. The thermometer dropped to forty degrees below zero, where it remained until the end of February. At times, the snow was so deep no one could see where he was going because there were no fences, roads, or trees to break the unbroken whiteness. Alice learned the meaning of snow blindness. The sun struggled to break through, but the wind whipped up loose snow until the air was blurred and it seemed as though snow was coming up out of the ground as well as down from the sky.

The cynical young husband where Alice lived had taunted her about her religion. He swore lustily to annoy her until she fled outside to sob in frustration and pray for forebearance and strength to carry on.

As the storm raged on, the supply of firewood gave out. It was necessary to burn some of the meager furniture to keep warm. An entire neighbor family froze to death. Animals died from cold and lack of food.

"Now, where's your God?" mocked the young man. "We're dying of hunger," he shouted angrily. "Why doesn't your God come to save us?"

There was no way to get to the nearest town, eighteen miles away. Food ran out until all that remained were some frozen potatoes and no way to thaw them. Only a cow and a horse remained in the barn.

At nightfall, they put on more clothes than they ever wore in the daytime to keep from freezing to death in their sleep. If there was fire enough to heat water to put into a hot water bottle, they would wake up the next morning to find a block of ice in the hot water bottle under the covers.

One day, Alice huddled near the stove trying to warm her near-frozen arms. She could see her breath over the top of the stove. She was unaware that her numb elbow was touching the stovepipe. When she did notice it, a large blister had formed. It would not heal until the storm had broken and she was able to get to a doctor for medical attention. The scar never disappeared.

Finally, in desperation, the young husband made his way to a neighbor, and the two men decided to try to get to town. Alice remained in the sod hut with the young wife. They put all the bedding on one bed and crawled in under the covers to try to keep warm while they waited.

Once they got up to stagger out to the barn to get water for the suffering horse and cow. In the brief twenty minutes outdoors, the calves of Alice's legs froze and it was agony thawing them with handfuls of snow.

When the two men did not return, the women remained in bed wondering if they would ever be warm again. Was this to be the end of life?

But the next morning, they looked out to see a dark blur on the horizon. It grew larger and took the shape of two men making their way through the storm. However, relief soon turned to dismay. The men only brought a tubful of coal and one frozen loaf of bread. Everything in town had been rationed.

Rescue planes had dropped packages of coal and food as they flew over the snowbound town, but the need far outstripped the supply.

A few days later the storm broke. Alice was able to take the horse to get to the Indian Mission Headquarters. Over much of the way, it was impossible to get any bearings; but the faithful horse avoided ditches and saved them from wandering in blind circles. When Alice finally reached the Mission Headquarters, she was given food and warm shelter until better weather permitted her return to her school.

During the storm, Alice wondered if she was ever to reach her goal as a missionary. Yet she did not cry out in self-pitying despair, asking why God allowed her to suffer so many difficulties. She gave thanks that she was alive.

After three years with the Sioux Indians in South Dakota, Alice went to Wyandotte, Oklahoma, to serve as pastor of a Quaker church among Seneca Indians.

She had barely settled at her new post when she was asked to conduct a funeral service. She had never attended a Quaker funeral, much less conducted one. She swallowed bravely, squared her slim shoulders, and did her best. After the service at the church, she was told to sit in front with the driver of the hearse on the way to the cemetery. When she saw the lettering on the side of the hearse, she held back a chuckle with difficulty. It read "Buzzard Funeral Company." Her situation was not eased when she climbed in beside the driver and noticed the heater at her feet. A picture of a red devil with forked tail and pointed ears leered out above a sign, "Red Devil Heater."

Alice worked in this Quaker church, and in a mission for the Kickapoo Indians, for a year before returning to the Hartford Seminary where she began her study for a Bachelor of Divinity Degree. She was convinced now that she needed this to carry out her goal on the foreign mission field. At first, she had struggled with the question of whether she wanted to be a pastor because of her father's dream for himself, or if she was doing it because she truly felt it was God who was calling her as a part of His call to the mission field. By now it had been almost ten years since that Sunday morning when she had announced her "calling" to her father. She had come to a deep sense of peace and could sincerely pray, "Father, I am ready to stay here in this country or go to another country as You wish. You have brought me through these experiences for a purpose, and I am ready to be fulfilled as You wish." To go back to the seminary was the next step in a plan that she felt was God's plan. She did not know how He would use these experiences, but she was sure they were valuable preparation for the future.

Years later, a friend was talking to her about the difficulties of being accepted by the Mission Board. "Didn't you offer to pay your own salary for the first two or three years? Your grandmother had left you something, and you had some meager savings from teaching."

Alice looked puzzled, then nodded. "Yes," she answered. "I had forgotten all about that."

Her first consideration had been service in a foreign country, and practical matters had slipped out of her thinking. It did not occur to her to dwell on thoughts of self-sacrifice; her one goal was clear, unwavering.

At the end of the second year of seminary, a letter came one day inviting her to go the New York office for an interview with the Methodist Board of Missions. It was on the eve of her final examinations. After the New York interview, she was told that she had been accepted. Would she be ready to leave for work in western China by the first of June? That was less than a week away.

She rushed back to the seminary, passed her examinations, then hurried to Iowa where her uncle was a Methodist minister. In the little rural church of Mount Etna, a member of the Mission Board commissioned her as a foreign missionary.

By the fourth of July, she was in California ready to board an ocean liner which was to take her far from her native land.

"She was as happy as a lark," her Aunt Tee reported later. She was on her way to the realization of her long-cherished dream.

And so it was that a great missionary was ready to begin her life's work. Her father's and her aunt's teachings were to hold her steady through experiences that tested both physical and spiritual stamina. A severe physical handicap, a near-fatal childhood illness, incredible hardships, the trial of raw jealousy, and confrontation with hostile challenges to her faith all contributed to severe but practical preparation for her life ahead.

Pruning the rose bush may seem to be severe. But it gives strength to the roots, promising a sturdy bush with lovelier blossoms in the time to come.

3
On the Way

It was a sunny fourth of July when her aunt and uncle took Alice to San Francisco to board the ship for China.

The dingy dock along the waterfront swarmed with bustling people. Passengers checked tickets and baggage at a desk at the foot of the gangplank, then made their way on board the *S. S. President Cleveland.* Derricks rumbled and groaned as they swung crates of cargo from the dock over and down into the ship's hold.

Alice bubbled with excitement. She waved from the deck to her aunt and uncle who had brought her to the ship. It slid out into the bay, and soon she was looking back over the stern to see the Golden Gate Bridge receding into the distance.

She was on her way! Her dream to live and work among people in a foreign land was coming true.

She knew no one on board, but she was soon enjoying other passengers and the ship's activities.

Her account in her letters to her Aunt Tee describes her experience:

"It doesn't seem like hundreds of miles from shore, but I guess I've gone too far to swim back. The sea is deep blue with white clouds along the horizon. My deck chair is on the back of the ship so I can see a good half circle of the horizon. People pace the deck with determination to make thirteen rounds, which add up to a mile.

"There are only about one hundred seventy-five passengers on board, so I have a chance to know most of them. I seem to be the only new missionary. One young couple is returning to India, another to Shanghai for the Seventh Day Adventist Mission.

"My roommate and I are getting along fine. Neither one of us is homesick or finds it difficult to make friends, so we don't depend on each other or get on each other's nerves. I've played ping-pong, shuffleboard, and checkers; but I haven't gone swimming in the funny-looking bath tub of a tiny swimming pool. There is lots to read, and everyone has something interesting to pass around. I have been enjoying my steamer letters and the exciting packages to be opened day by day.

"I saw the ship's doctor about cholera and smallpox shots and have stocked up on quinine.

"Tonight we have the captain's dinner and tomorrow we dock in Honolulu. We get in about noon and leave at midnight . . . I'll wear my new dress. I had my hair done. It cost me $2.25, but I guess it was worth it to be a good representative of my family . . .

"There is a caressing breeze blowing with more whitecaps than we have seen since leaving San Francisco. The sea has a blueing color, and I never tire of watching its ceaseless activity . . . I've had a great time watching the flying fish. They look like little birds that suddenly emerge from waves and glide from one wave crest to another.

"Last night the Adventists and Baptists had a huge sing while the rest played a horse race gambling game . . . I don't want to give a wrong impression of missionaries. The Methodists didn't gamble, but they were not conspicuous in their separation from the rest of the passengers. I watched everything with interest. My roommate is Catholic, making the trip for pleasure; but we have good times together and don't seem to misunderstand each other.

"We had a good discussion at the table this noon. I am the only missionary at my table, and the others started asking me questions about comparative religions and attitudes of people in different countries. They seemed to be sincerely interested. I'm no authority and didn't pose as one.

"An albatross has been following us all the way. He looks so lonesome all by himself. Yesterday we had a fire drill. We all had to get life belts and report to our assigned boat stations. We looked so funny in those white jackets that fit like barrels . . .

"We have a little paper giving news. The international situation doesn't look too good. I wonder what will happen by the time I reach Shanghai. There is a French Catholic priest on board returning to French Indo-China, and he doesn't know how he will be able to go on from Manila.

"The ship's bells tell the time and are a mystery to me. When it is time for meals, a steward comes around with some chimes and calls the meals; but I haven't learned to count the ship's bells for the hour."

There were many interesting passengers on board. Alice, like many others, was curious about a few mysterious characters who made sure that no one knew anything about their backgrounds or destinations. She was delighted to make the acquaintance of Dr. and Mrs. Sam Higgenbottom of the famous Presbyterian Mission in India, and Dr. and Mrs. Foley of the Union Church and Cooperative in the Philippines.

In Honolulu, a group from the ship spent the six hours in port in a hired car which took them over much of the island. Alice was delighted with the lush tropical growth everywhere.

It was 1940 and China was at war with Japan. Word came that their ship would not be allowed to stop at the designated port of Shanghai, China. They were to be put ashore in Yokohama, Japan. After spending the night there, they would continue their journey on a Canadian ship.

When they were to drop anchor in Yokohama harbor, Alice exchanged some of her American money for Japanese yen with the ship's barber. She had no idea that it was illegal. When inspectors came aboard, she innocently answered their questions; and the barber was arrested and taken off the ship.

"You've killed the barber!" someone shouted as she went ashore. Badly upset, she felt a combination of guilt and a fear bordering on panic. However, she later learned that the barber had been released unharmed.

A Presbyterian missionary from the ship helped her into a rickshaw. It was to take her to the hotel where the passengers were to spend the night.

In her human-drawn chair, Alice and her rickshaw puller quickly melted into the crowds of kimono-clad Japanese. Japanese shops lined the narrow streets with signs in incomprehensible hieroglyphics. Vendors hawked wares carried in baskets at the end of poles slung across their shoulders.

A Japanese policeman emerged out of the throng to stop Alice's rickshaw. She was terrified. What could be wrong now? She neither spoke nor understood Japanese, or their laws or customs. How could she explain that she was only an American traveler staying overnight in this strange city?

After much gesticulating and noisy discussion between the policeman and the rickshaw puller, they were told to go on their way. The policeman, Alice finally understood, was only looking for cigarettes.

She heaved a sigh of relief. Then it occurred to her that she knew nothing about her rickshaw puller. She was entirely in his power. He might take her anywhere, and she had no way of communicating with him or asking for help from a passerby.

It was a blisteringly hot day, and the puller stopped to mop his brow. With a friendly grin, he looked around at her and remarked in good English, "It's a hot day, isn't it?"

That evening, Alice joined three other women from the ship for a sight-seeing taxi drive around the city. Each of them enjoyed a private room in a comfortable hotel for the night. Every room had its own bath with a maid to draw the water and turn back the bed.

The window of Alice's room opened on a spectacular view of the harbor. The next morning, she caught a glimpse through the early morning mist of majestic Fujiyama. Below her window some sort of military training was going on. Soon, recruits all left in long lines of brown cars and trucks.

Out on the street she admired the pretty kimonos some people wore and discovered that many spoke English. She paid eight cents for a rickshaw ride back to the waterfront, where she became acquainted with quarantine and immigration proceedings, then boarded the *S.S. Empress of Russia* for Shanghai.

When the ship stopped at Nagasaki, Japan, to load coal, Alice saw a living picture of fountains and islands rising out of blue, blue water. Picturesque boats and houses filled the foreground. How could man-made poverty, filth, and disease exist in a setting of such beauty! She observed some of that man-made power substituting for machinery as coal was loaded into the ship's hold by long lines of women, children, and a few men. They carried heavy baskets from small boats at the side of the ship.

Evidences of war appeared on board. Guns bristled fore and aft, and special precautions were made for black-outs and the use of life jackets. Alice's roommate this time was going to Chengtu to teach English in the Gin Ling College. They had much to talk about.

A hundred miles before they sighted land, the blue ocean water became a dirty yellow from the Yangtse River.

At last, some eight miles up the river from the ocean, their liner entered the port of Shanghai.

4
China at Last

When they docked, Alice made her way down the unsteady gangplank to step ashore in the bustling city of Shanghai. She had read, heard, and seen pictures of China; and this milling throng of almond-eyed humanity shouting, hurrying, busy with dockside activities offered an exciting introduction to the life before her.

She looked about hopefully; but preoccupied with their own affairs, nobody was paying attention to this eager young American in her conspicuously foreign clothes. The steward from the ship set her luggage on the dock, accepted the tip she had been coached to give him, bowed his thanks, and hurried away.

Nearby, loose-jacketed coolies stood between the shafts of their rickshaws shouting invitations to accept their transportation. Cries of vendors shrilled along the dock. Sampans bobbed cheerfully at the water's edge, and the rumbling of the unloading machinery bringing cargo up from the ship's hold echoed the noise of the San Francisco and Yokohama docks.

Alice's heart pounded. What should she do? She thought she must look like a brooding hen as she tried to spread out over her suitcases and trunk. Eager, pushing coolies clustered about to snatch everything they could carry to load into rickshaws.

The daughter of a missionary who had been with Alice on the ship appeared out of the throng. "Wait here," she said. "I'll call the Methodist Mission, and they'll send someone to get you."

A short time later, she heard an American voice in the din and looked up to see the welcome face of a fellow countryman. "We're so sorry," he said breathlessly. "We didn't receive word of your arrival." The letter had come on the boat with her.

At that time, foreign countries had special zones in Shanghai. When the missionary and his wife took Alice to a meeting at the church that evening, they passed through the barrier between the Japanese occupied area and the foreign concessions. When they were stopped for inspection, Alice had her first encounter with the inconvenience, often threats, of wartime inspection and restrictions. She was to experience many more in the months, even years, ahead.

Shanghai was a modern city. Its population included thousands of people from countries all over the world. Guns, soldiers, and armored cars mingled with swarms of underfed people in rags. Many had been bombed out of their homes and had no place to live but on the city streets. The task of helping so many needy people seemed staggering, but the churches were making heroic efforts to meet the critical needs.

It was unsafe to be on the streets at night, especially if one had any appearance of opulence. However, Alice met a modest young Chinese woman in her twenties who calmly went into one of the worst sections of the city to work with children. She wore a badge for identification when alone at night, and no one troubled her.

The three weeks in Shanghai were crowded with meeting new friends, visiting points of interest, and preparing for what was to be a long and unexpectedly difficult journey. She would need a small stove, canned heat, and eating utensils, as well as additional passport visas.

She visited several churches, all of them behind walls. Only a gate or door appeared on the street, but inside there were often spacious courts and growing flowers. She took the train and rickshaw trip to see Nanking University and was sprayed coming and going by Japanese police with disinfectant. She saw the famous Gin Ling College with its beautiful campus and tradition of tragedy and heroism in providing new opportunites for Chinese girls and women. A day's bicycle trip with two University instructors took her into the country, and she had her first glimpse of a Chinese countryside with its farms, villages, silk industry, and shrines.

She learned that there was no transportation by plane or boat to her destination of Chengtu in far western China. There were no roads. China was a vast land of rugged mountains and sea level plains. Great distances had to be covered by primitive carts if there were paths, or by junks on winding waterways. For centuries, the mighty Yangtse River had offered the only way to reach the far western province of Szechwan. The road to Szechwan, it was said, was as difficult as the road to Heaven.

She met Pearl Fosnot, a veteran missionary, who was to travel with her. Short, good-natured Pearl possessed the seasoned wisdom of one who ordered her life with unfailing good judgment. She was an ideal traveling companion. She knew China and the Chinese, spoke the language fluently, and was experienced in meeting the problems of getting about under difficult conditions. She was to take Alice to the province of Szechwan where she would attend the language school in Chengtu.

Because of the war with Japan, they were told, every means of travel, even the most primitive, was booked "for years ahead." Finally, they were able to get passage south on a freighter to the English city of Hong Kong. Baggage limitations held each traveler to one hundred twenty-five pounds, which included bedding, suitcases, and whatever could be crowded into a dufflebag. All else had to be left in Shanghai.

Late one evening, they boarded the freighter, and after four days of travel along the Pacific coast, they arrived in beautiful Hong Kong. The view from the harbor was spectacular. Green hills rose out of the bay. With characteristic imagination, Alice wrote her aunt that the "houses are built all the way to the top and look as though someone had taken a handful of pretty pictures and pasted them against a green wall." A little cable car crawled to the top, and Alice felt like "a fly who would fall off the wall if she didn't hang on to the bushes along the way."

The top of the hill commanded a view of glittering Hong Kong spread out below. The bay was spotted with little freight junks where scores of Chinese were born, lived, and died. The "new territory" could be seen on the mainland in the distance.

Alice and Pearl learned that every means of travel from Hong Kong to western China also was booked "for years ahead." They began to think of trying to slip through the Japanese lines on foot when word came that a French freighter was going to Haiphong, from where they could re-enter China and make connections with the railway to Kunming.

Alice was startled to see the varied assortment of passengers on board. Representing a wide spectrum of nationalities, vocations, and personalities, some were unlike any people she had ever encountered before.

One overweight, balding Frenchman loudly

proclaimed his ideas on any and all topics. "The only way to survive in this forsaken place," he declaimed aggressively, waving his glass of beer to emphasize his remarks, "is to drown all the germs in booze." Alice wondered if he might drown himself along with the germs.

When they arrived in Haiphong, they had yet to make their way back into China, which they had left when going to Hong Kong. The only other ship in sight in the Haiphong harbor was a Japanese gunboat, ominously leveling its guns on the arriving travelers. All passengers of the French freighter were hurried ashore without any delay for baggage inspection. The Japanese had delivered an ultimatum and might move in at any moment to take everyone prisoner.

Even in their hurry, Alice was to notice that every city offered something of interest. In Haiphong, people were proud of their black teeth. They chewed bettle nuts until their lips were a bright red and their teeth coal black. They regarded life with an eerie black smile, poor subjects for a toothpaste ad. Their hair was threaded through strips of cloth wound around their heads like long braids. Some hair usually straggled out loosely, but did not detract from the colorful and becoming style. Women's dresses were slit from the waist on the sides over long white trousers. People carried burdens on their heads instead of their shoulders or in their arms. Market day brought mountain tribes into town wearing bright-colored skirts and blouses with grass ornaments.

The next morning, Alice and Pearl boarded a train going north from Haiphong. The roadbed was a marvel of engineering genius. Making its way over and through towering mountains, it crossed deep gorges and rushing rivers. Bombed-out bridges forced frequent stops where passengers left the train to cross on an improvised bridge on foot. Another train awaited them on the other side.

At every station, soldiers were waiting for transportation; and there was no predicting when Alice and Pearl might be left stranded, because soldiers took over the train.

In spite of the danger and uncertainties, the trip offered the rewards of beautiful scenery. From sea-level Haiphong, to the mountains with their heads in the clouds, the train made its way past banana trees, tropical flowers, and matted jungle too dense to admit even a narrow path.

When they finally reached Kunming in China, the railroad bridge had been mined by the Chinese, ready to be blown up if the Japanese arrived. The train cautiously crawled over the bridge, followed by a second train carrying baggage and freight. As soon as the last car of the second train had cleared the bridge, it suddenly exploded into the air, leaving only a yawning chasm where they had just crossed.

As they entered Kunming, only dim bulbs at infrequent intervals lighted the narrow streets. Old, uneven cobblestones left holes in the street where stagnant water remained in puddles. People threw all manner of waste into the gutters, where they also bathed and washed their teeth.

A solid line of shops opened on the street in daytime. A wall like a folding door shut them off at night. People made many of their wares as they "minded the store." If they put out mushrooms or pottery to dry on the sidewalk, passersby merely walked around them out into the street.

The owner of a little restaurant or shop might carry his business on a pole across his shoulder. He would put it down somewhere and open for business. He might have something to make a shrill noise to announce that he was ready for customers.

Some people, as well as their little pack burros,

seemed to be well fed; but tattered rags hung loosely on the gaunt frames of others. Alice saw a beggar picking up grains of rice dropped from a torn sack by someone coming from the railroad. She was told that the standard of living was measured by the cost of rice.

The street presented the uninviting side of living. The beautiful and clean were kept for private enjoyment inside the home, shut away from the filthy, odorous street. Alice watched a ragged little old lady with bound feet hobbling along with an armload of flowers she had bought, probably from a street vendor. It would grace her sheltered home, however humble it might be.

The beautifully carved gates of the city seemed to rise out of the noise and dirt like a misplaced treasure from an art gallery.

Alice learned that more than half of the women of middle age and older had bound feet. Foot binding had been officially banned in 1911, but the old idea that tiny, deformed feet were beautiful had persisted. But now, Alice saw no pathetic little girl sobbing in a doorway unable to run and play with other children because of the anguish of cruelly bound little feet.

Children, especially girls, were sometimes sold into slavery. A mission in Kunming cared for those they could rescue. Two former slave girls in the mission were studying to be Bible women. Because of the frequent air raids, the mission was moving to the safety of the country.

Alice and Pearl visited a German Sisters' school for the blind. Sixty students had come from various parts of China. Their support came from England and local people. When two little girls sang, they raised their sightless eyes to the sky and threw back their shoulders as if they had all the joy in the world.

Outside of the drab, crowded city, beautiful parks

graced the scene. Alice and Pearl visited the lovely campus of Yonan University. They went to the Quaker Mission and helped prepare candy for two hundred college students. A mission outing was held in one of the parks under a full moon. People worshiped, played games, told jokes, and enjoyed refreshments much like similar groups in America.

Between three and four thousand students from all the colleges, as well as two armies of more than 20,000 young soldiers, were located in Kunming. Later, many of the students were moved to greater safety from the fighting with the Japanese.

Alice and Pearl stayed in a Chinese mission house built around three courts. A Bible school for children trained leaders, who lived in one court. The chapel and gate occupied another, and workers lived in a third court. The windows were covered with paper and the walls were thin wood. Everyone could hear everyone else, until there seemed to be no privacy even for one's own thoughts.

Typically, gay growing flowers and beautiful carvings provided a cozy mission house setting inside but presented a blank wall to the dirty, muddy streets outside.

Mail came through fairly regularly. Alice wished that she might have been posted in a letter. She would have arrived in much less time than it was taking her to reach Chengtu.

One day she joined others from the Mission for a trip across a nearby lake. Fishing birds came alongside to dive for fish and gobble them as they swam. Alice made her first acquaintance with Chinese cormorants. With strings tied around their necks, the huge birds would catch fish to be taken out for a human meal before their necks were freed to dive again for their own dinner.

The excursionists followed a long canal bordered

by rice fields. Alice enjoyed the lark of helping to row the boat. It was three times the size of an ordinary American rowboat, and she had to stand to get the full swing of the long oars. She returned to the city with sore muscles, a stiff back, and a happy memory of an unusual experience.

Many owners lived on their boats. Their only possessions were the boat, the clothes on their backs, and in one end of the boat, a little mud stove with an iron skillet. They might have a roll of bedding under a mat.

Travel conditions were so uncertain and hazardous that Alice and Pearl had to remain a month in Kunming. They had arrived at the Burma Road where hundreds of Americans and thousands of Chinese had toiled in the scorching sun and drenching rain to build the vital supply route of 2,100 miles from Rangoon to Chungking to truck supplies into China from the outside world.

The Japanese held the China port cities, and all cargo had to be brought through India and Burma. Laborers on the road, which had only been completed in 1939, suffered from dysentery and malaria, as well as the miseries of mosquitoes and other insects and discomforts. There was never enough of anything for the work or for human comfort and hygiene. Planes overhead were flying the "hump" under makeshift conditions in craft ill-equipped for the dangerous journey.

It was a difficult time and place for the civilian traveler. Alice and Pearl had to accept the routine of daily air raids. They were regularly driven indoors, or if there was time for a warning, out through the city gates into the fields beyond the city wall.

One day Alice and Pearl were talking with a Chinese shopkeeper when they heard the signal for an air raid. A white flag, they knew, bearing the figure of a red airplane was being hung on every police station, and policemen were riding through the city with similar flags on their bicycles.

Everyone was hurrying about in the streets. Alice and Pearl had gone about a block when the siren blew for the first signal to leave the city. They asked a policeman trying to direct traffic if they would have time to reach the mission where they were staying. When he assured them there was time, they dodged through the crowds of people carrying bags and bundles.

Some looked worried. Others laughed and joked. Babies had been grabbed up in blankets to be carried on children's or mother's backs. Two or three cars rushed by honking hysterically. Swarms of rickshaws followed.

By the time Alice and Pearl reached the mission, the second alarm sounded. It meant that enemy planes were in sight and everyone should take cover wherever possible. It was too late to rush outside the city gates to the safety of the country. Because of the flat, damp ground inside the city, there were few underground bomb shelters. Chinese scout planes could be heard overhead, too high to be seen. From the mission court they saw eighteen Japanese planes flying in formation and heard the roar of their engines punctuated by the putt-putt-putt of anti-aircraft fire. Clouds of smoke marked locations of bomb explosions.

Everyone at the mission hid under furniture for protection from falling shrapnel. They heard the crash of a bomb nearby. When they looked out ten minutes later, only smoke was to be seen as they heard the drone of departing planes.

Alice was too excited to be frightened. It seemed like a bad dream. After four hours, when the all-clear siren sounded, the daily routine continued as usual.

At the time of another air raid they remained in the city to avoid the crush of fleeing people trying to get through the city gates. Alice saw a bomb fall a couple of blocks away. She joined Pearl and rushed indoors, grabbing the nearest object at hand. They ducked their heads under overturned chair backs.

When the bombing stopped, Alice looked down to see what she had been holding for protection. It was a soft bundle of gauzy mosquito netting! She burst out laughing. Even with the danger and tense uncertainty, a chuckle was ready to bubble to the surface over the ridiculous.

The two travelers attended a Methodist church early one Sunday morning, an Episcopal service later. With her own English prayer book Alice was able to follow the Chinese service. She went to an evening service in the large chapel of the mission where they were staying.

Before the evening program began, a student and the pastor of the church stood at the door; and, as people passed in the street, they were invited to join the service. A sizable group gathered, the women on one side of the room, the men on the other.

It was a varied group. Ragged beggars mixed with students and shopkeepers. A mother had a baby strapped to her back. A man held the little fist of a small boy. They all listened with interest to the minister's message and quickly learned the chorus of some of the hymns. When the people were told how to act during prayer, the room was silent and all heads were bowed. Some remained afterward to talk with the leaders of the meeting. Alice had attended similar meetings in America, but here many knew nothing about the Bible, prayer, and the basic tenets of Christianity.

The weather was warm in the sun, cool in the shade. At night a blanket was welcome. Cooking was done with charcoal, which gave off little or no smoke. Alice enjoyed making peanut brittle over a charcoal fire from native sugar that come in little cakes, like maple sugar in America.

With a good climate, seeds dropped in the rich soil grew with little attention. Farmers raised fruit and vegetables the year around.

The consul came one day to say that all women and children were to be out of the city by the next day. That night, a Chinese truck driver appeared saying he was taking a load of Goodyear tires over the Burma Road to Chungking. When he told Alice and Pearl that they might ride in the cab of the truck with him, they gladly accepted. For two weeks, the three of them dodged bombs dropped along the famous road. Whether in villages or open country, they were in constant danger.

The countryside began to look less and less strange to Alice as they drove day after day by rice fields dotted with plodding water buffalo. They survived on delicious Chinese food and stayed in Chinese inns of varying degrees of cleanliness and comfort.

At last, they saw the city of Chungking in the distance. A wave of joy swept over them. They had reached the province of Szechwan where Alice's work was to be. After weeks of uncertainty and frustration, they were nearing the end of their long, hazardous journey. It was Sunday. Perhaps they could reach the church and give thanks for their safe arrival.

But, unhappily, just then the truck broke down. They would have to wait by the roadside until a new part could be brought from the city. Their only food was hot sweet potatoes brought by kind farmers, and they were convinced that no food had ever tasted so good.

A rainbow arched across the sky reflecting its

glorious colors in the quiet waters of the rice fields below. Its promise gave hope and inspiration to the weary travelers. They walked up and down the road as the western sun was enthroned in a red mantel of fluffy clouds of pastel shades. The hills seemed to be covered with a carpet stretching to the horizon. When the sun set, the glow in the western sky stirred feelings of peace and contentment. The hymn, "Day Is Dying in the West," almost sang itself. It was always to have special meaning for Alice in the years that followed.

By nightfall the truck was repaired, and they continued on into Chungking. On arrival, they found the Methodist church. The building had been badly damaged by bombs, but a meeting was in progress as usual. Pearl enjoyed a happy reunion with missionary friends, and Alice met some of the colleagues with whom she would have much in common in the difficult and dangerous days ahead.

The trip from Kunming had taken fifteen days. After a week in Chungking, they were on their way to their final destination of Chengtu. The university truck provided their transportation on this last lap of their journey. It burned alcohol instead of gasoline, and limped and spurted through villages and past farms. They stopped along the way to visit mission stations with their busy schools and churches.

Flowers bloomed everywhere: roses, marigolds, violets, narcissus, chrysanthemums, and salvia. Their gay blossoms belonged to summer; but when the sun disappeared behind clouds, the air felt like winter. The hint of fall appeared in the yellow leaves of the ginkgo trees. Everyone was wearing woolens, and Alice was glad that her one hundred twenty-five pounds of baggage had allowed for some heavy clothes — along with her typewriter.

Then one evening, the truck stopped at a gate in a

wall. Was she dreaming? Could it be that she had finally arrived?

It was two days less than four months since her ship had sailed out through the Golden Gate of San Francisco. She felt the beginning of a sense of fulfillment. Treacherous travel, danger of war bombs, and incredible physical discomforts had not dampened her zeal for what she had dedicated her life to do.

5
Language School and War

The city of Chengtu was the capital of the west China province of Szechwan. It had attracted world wide attention when faculty and students of the University of Nanking had escaped Japanese invaders by loading their books, laboratory equipment, and personal possessions on their backs to carry on foot 2000 miles inland. At Chengtu, they continued their academic program, eventually setting up a hospital in connection with their school of medicine. Wu-yi-Fan, president of the famous Gingling College, also moved her entire institution to the safety of Chengtu.

Chengtu was situated on a level plain stretching out as far as the mist allowed visibility. On a clear day after a rain, the Himalaya Mountains stood out in all their snowy majesty for a full half-circle on the horizon three hundred miles away. A corner of the city wall climbed abruptly to the top of a hill crowned by a pagoda. Behind the pagoda, steep mountains reached upward.

The district offices of the Methodist Mission were located in Chengtu. The language school for missionaries maintained living quarters for single students in a large two-story building. Married couples sometimes lived with the missionaries. Alice stayed with a Chinese family for a time, then with the

Stockwell family, long-time effective leaders in the mission program. Students bicycled across the city to study Chinese.

Teachers at the school knew no English. They taught on a one-to-one basis, as well as in classes.

"You must learn as a child learns," Alice's teacher began through an interpreter. "The child does not read or write. He listens. You must listen and speak."

Alice was surprised to discover that without spelling and grammatical structure, Chinese offered advantages as well as difficulties. It was disconcerting to learn that she would need to know at least six hundred characters if she were to have even a minimum skill in reading and writing. It was to be very much later, when she was bedridden with mumps, that she took up further study and learned that reading and writing were far more difficult than speaking Chinese. While attending the language school, her class in Chinese history reviewed much that she had learned in the Hartford seminary.

Of the nine language students in her class, one was Canadian, one Chinese (of another province where they spoke a different dialect), and another an American. They represented various church denominations: Baptist, Methodist, English Anglican, and Quaker.

Her teacher was a wrinkled little man in a dark skull cap and glasses. A single hair protruded aggressively from his chin. Sitting motionless in his loose blue Chinese jacket and baggy trousers, he exemplified characteristic Chinese imperturbability. His personal dignity, serene good humor and wit, as well as his never-failing courtesy, were typical, Alice was to learn, not only of the Chinese scholar, but also of the humblest coolie. Tucking his hands in his sleeves, he would bow low when his students entered and left his class.

Alice would think that she was making progress learning Chinese. Then she would discover that she could communicate with her teacher; but when she tried to talk with anyone outside the classroom, she was jolted into a realization that she had a long, long way to go with a language so dissimilar to her own.

There was much to learn about China as well as the Chinese language. The country was too vast for casual generalizations. Customs, climate, even dialects varied. Modern industry clustered along the coastal areas where transportation and communication were developing more rapidly than in the remote western provinces.

She studied the economy, sociology, and educational systems of her adopted country. She explored various resources, including materials of the government educational bureau. The Mission worked closely with several government social programs. A Farmers' Cooperative held monthly meetings to promote the welfare and interests of the farmers. Women's groups met twice a year to hear speakers on methods for improving their domestic skills. A Bureau of Opium Suppression worked to eliminate the evils of opium use.

Agriculture Fairs were something like county fairs in the United States. Farmers brought their vegetables, chickens, and goats, while the women displayed samples of handcrafts and home-prepared foods. A contest named the healthiest baby.

Boy Scouts and Girl Scouts, sponsored by the government, helped with public functions and directed traffic at festivals. Their meetings closely resembled those of their brothers and sisters across the sea. One marked difference appeared in the omission from their pledge of the words "under God." 4-H Clubs encouraged future farmers to increase their knowledge and improve their skills. Some limited their program to one subject, such as a boys' club named the Goat Club.

The Chamber of Commerce sponsored parades. Merchants usually shared in the costs of fireworks, floats, and skits of classic scenes and stories. Sometimes men dressed as idols from the temples, were carried through the streets.

Eighty percent of all work done in China was associated with agriculture. Crops included many kinds of vegetables and cereals as well as silk, sugar cane, and cotton. Rice was a major crop, especially in the south; wheat was more frequently raised in the north.

Most farms were too small for large machinery and such equipment would have been prohibitively expensive. Human labor was plentiful and cheap. In Szechwan, women worked beside their husbands in the fields. It was common to see a father with a baby strapped on his back as he bent over the rice planting, or a mother with her baby on her back beside her husband.

Three-fourths of the domestic animals were used for draft, but ten percent of the farms had no work animals at all. Every home had a pig — even in the towns and cities. The Chinese word for "home" is made up of the word for "pig" under the word for "roof." If you have food and shelter, you have a home. Chickens were also a common part of the household. The Buddhist teaching held that since the cows and buffalo were the work animals, they should not provide food also; therefore, even milk for food was frowned upon as an insult to the cow. The Mohammedans of the community would not eat pork, but ate beef and used the hides. There seemed to be no great discord in this difference in belief as each person followed any part of any religion that seemed to be effective.

Human excrement was carefully collected and used for fertilizer. Intestinal parasites entered the human system through the bare feet of the farmers working in this "night soil."

Alice had grown up on a farm, but there was little resemblance to what she had known in her girlhood to what she now saw all about her. No helpful government pamphlets or farm agent offered aid or hope of relief from grinding poverty. There was an ever-present threat of hunger, pestilence, flood, or drought.

On a trip out into the country, Alice saw the continually changing patterns of wheat, vegetables, mustard, indigo, cotton, rice, beans, fruit trees, and peanuts. Fields were broken here and there by groups of mounds indicating graves. These were above ground with no headstones. Often paper decorations mounted on sticks marked the burial spot. Alice saw a man lighting incense and red candles at one of the graves.

Little shrines by the roadside or in a field sheltered tiny stone idols with sticks of half-burned incense in front of them. Here and there a slowly plodding water buffalo pulled a primitive plow. Clumps of trees framed fields or red-tiled roofed farm houses.

Floods, drought, and soil erosion contributed to irrigation difficulties. Terraced hillsides held back water, prevented erosion and simplified cultivation, but pests were prevalent.

Alice had heard of the remarkable irrigation system in western China. She saw ditches and river beds being newly dug or repaired for incoming water.

Legend told of a man named Li Bin about 300 B.C., in the time of the Chin dynasty. He saw the marshy land on one side of the mountain and the dry, bare land on the other side. He planned the system to make sure that both sides had adequate water for their crops. He cut through the mountain where his temple now stood and "put iron in the bottom of the river." He also worked out the plans for keeping the ditches clean. His son carried on after him; and annually, for over two thousand years, these plans had been followed. They had been so effective that no one had seen any necessity for change. It had been the only place in all of China where irrigation provided success in flood control. Even the canals in the east could not compare with it.

Some believed that the primitive tribespeople built and maintained the system before the Chinese conquered them and took it over. Much of the maintenance was still carried on by the descendants of the tribespeople. The entire province of Szechwan was laced with waterways replenished each spring from the melted snow from nearby mountains.

Every year the "opening of the waters" was celebrated with the sacrifice of a pig, a meat fast, and an elaborate ceremony. Scantily clad young men went down the street as bystanders dashed water on them to the sound of drums and gongs.

Alice was impressed by the intelligent planning of people considered to be primitive. A dam in the river was constructed of baskets made of bamboo rope and filled with rocks. They were so placed that a man on the bank could pull a bamboo rope and the entire dam would fall apart, letting the river water flow into the canal.

Alice became acquainted with many Mission programs. She attended a service in the Baptist church located near a section of the city burned out in a recent bombing raid. The congregation included people of various denominations. One of the language students led the service, and President Wu of the Gin Ling College spoke.

After the service, she went to see the dormitory where Pearl Fosnot lived on the Gin Ling campus. Later, a missionary doctor conducted an evening service, and Alice was pleased to discover that she could understand many Chinese words. She had picked up more than she had realized in her travels with Pearl. She recognized most of the hymns by words as well as by the tunes.

She needed a bicycle to get across town from her living quarters to the language school, but they were difficult to find. When she located a second-hand one, it needed new tires, a new wheel brake, new pedals, a bell, and a carrier. She considered herself lucky to be able to buy it and set about putting it in shape with her own mechanical skill.

Dr. Peter Shih was dean of the Union Seminary in Chengtu. Alice had met him at Hartford where he had been one of the "gang" that had planned to go to Tibet. During the Boxer uprising in 1900, some enemies of the Shih family decided to kill all Shihs who were Christians. The Boxers were not anti-Christian so much as opposed to anything or anyone associated with a foreign country. Before the rebellion was quelled, the eldest son of Reverend Shih, Sr. was killed. Pastor Shih knew the identity of the man responsible for his son's death. When all of the Boxer leaders later were to be executed, he went to the government and asked that the man's life be spared. He took him into his home and converted him to Christianity. He became a minister and later a bishop of the Chinese church.

A second son of Pastor Shih was killed by robbers. Again, the father converted the murderers and helped them to learn to make an honest living. The one remaining son was Dr. Peter Shih. He was dean of the theological seminary when Alice arrived in Chengtu. He was working to help young people become self-supporting while getting an education. His wife was well educated, as was later his son. Alice stayed with the Shih family part of the time that she was attending the language school.

Some time after her arrival in Chengtu, word came that some of her baggage had reached Chungking. However, there had been serious bombing raids there upsetting all traffic in and out of the city. Chungking was nearer than Shanghai but there was no assurance that her wandering luggage would ever reach her. Finally, after eleven months on the way, it caught up with her. Since it included much that she needed in her work, it was a relief to join forces with it again.

Alice acquired some silk worms. She watched them grow and begin to spin as they fed on mulberry leaves. They increased about eight times in size in a week. Chinese women sometimes "wore" the eggs close to their bodies for warmth to speed their hatching. Alice, however, preferred a less intimate arrangement.

She had loved animals since her childhood on her father's farm and was delighted when a missionary returned from a trip to a bamboo forest with a large, six-month-old panda. It was to be sent to America as a gift from Madame Chiang. It had free run of the screened porch at the Mission and slept most of the day. Its diet consisted of cornmeal and milk. Although caught in a wild country, it was friendly and trusting. Alice delighted in watching it but avoided the long claws used to uncover bamboo shoots.

There was always something to see of interest. One day, Alice stopped to watch some acrobats performing in an open space left from a bombing raid. A circle of passersby had gathered to watch sword dancing and twirling balls on ropes while listening to funny stories. It cost the onlookers nothing. The performers made their living from the coins tossed to them after their acts.

Time moved on rapidly, and Alice began to feel a sense of belonging in her adopted country.

6
Land of Diversity

Alice was soon aware that she had come to a vast country with wide diversities of speech, products, even dress. But there was a growing effort to maintain law and order.

She looked out one day to see three men being taken outside of the city wall to be shot. One had been a robber; the other two had been involved in the opium traffic. China was making progress against the insidious, destructive use of opium. A few years before it had been estimated that twenty percent of the population took opium; it had been reduced to five percent.

Banditry afflicted the countryside, but when the thieves were caught, justice came swiftly and surely. Though slow and not always consistent, progress was evident.

At first, it seemed that the Chinese were unaware of the serious lack of sanitation. On closer acquaintance, however, it was apparent that much was being done to try to avoid the dangers of disease. Many people no longer used the same water to wash their faces as they used to wash their feet. Before and after a meal the diner would be given a hot towel whether in a hotel or a private residence. When people learned of better rules of cleanliness, they were meticulous in observing them.

Food was thoroughly cooked and served piping hot. It usually could be safely eaten in whatever surroundings. Newcomers, however, with no immunity to the local food, water, and other unavoidable risks, faced various health hazards. Alice was sensible about taking precautions, following a carefully balanced diet, and getting adequate exercise.

Blind, crippled, and desperately ill people appeared everywhere. They suffered from malnutrition, goiter, venereal disease, and innumerable other afflictions often too hideous to describe. In spite of annual inoculations for typhoid, smallpox, and (every few months) for cholera, illness struck with tragic speed.

Daily experiences were acquainting Alice with the remarkable people she was coming to admire and enjoy. One day, she set out on her bicycle down the cobble-stoned city streets. When she asked directions for reaching her destination, she managed the questions but was unable to understand the answers. Finally, an obliging policeman took pity on her and sloshed ahead down the muddy street to show the way. She was becoming acquainted with the characteristic courtesy and good nature of the Chinese.

Another well-known trait was "saving face." No one must suffer the loss of personal dignity. When she was having dinner in the home of Chinese friends, the chicken stew appeared on the table with only one leg and one wing. The hostess went to the kitchen and returned to report that the cook claimed that the chicken had been so tender in cooking, the leg and wing had melted away. The cook had followed the common practice of the "squeeze" and took for granted that servants would appropriate part of whatever they handled.

As China continued at war with Japan, bombs were the order of sunny days and moonlit nights. People in Chengtu lived under the constant threat of war's destruction. Public schools and schools for the children of missionaries had moved to the safety of distant rural areas.

However, anxiety was overshadowed by the happiness at last of being where Alice could learn the language and start her chosen life's work. She began to feel at home.

One day she started on a trip to visit some of the relocated schools. One of the missionaries helped her hire a whagger, a chair slung on two horizontal poles over the shoulders of two men. One carrier trotted in front of the passenger, another behind. The carriers were told that Alice knew very little Chinese.

They had not gone far when Alice became distressed by the heavy pressure of the whagger poles on the men's shoulders. She urged them to let her walk, but they only grunted and trotted on. The carrier in front talked continuously to the man behind her, explaining, she learned later, where they were turning, the condition of the road or path ahead, and suggesting the speed they should travel. An example: The front one warned, "Here comes the man." The back carrier answered: "He won't bite."

They came to a village and stopped to rest. No one had advised her not to travel in Western dress. American short skirts and sleeves, with generous displays of legs and arms, were considered indecent, even immoral. Female anatomy in China was well hidden inside high-necked, long-sleeved jackets and ankle-length slit skirts. Alice's clothes, as well as her blue eyes and freckles, brought a throng of excited villagers to see this strange foreigner.

It was a hot day and swarms of people crowded

around her. The more she tried to communicate with them, the more they chattered and laughed in amusement. They took the bobby pins out of her hair and fingered her dress, even trying to see what she wore underneath. They attempted to get behind her to see the tail they were sure she had hidden somewhere. She backed against a building to hold her skirts down and noticed that there were people on the roofs peering down at her.

Alice was frightened. She realized that she might unwittingly do something to violate a local custom and anger the crowd. She took her Testament out of her pocket and it fell open to Mark's account of the feeding of the five thousand. The thought came to her that, like the disciples on that well-known occasion, in the confusion of a noisy crowd, she felt assured that God would take care of her, using whatever limited resources she had.

She closed her eyes and prayed for guidance. When she opened them, people were staring at her in silence. With gestures someone asked her what she was doing. When she answered, also with gestures, that she was reading the Bible, they were interested but puzzled. They asked what the book said and she tried to tell them. She could not know how much they understood, but their attitude had changed. They were listening. As the carriers picked up her chair and started out of town, the crowd followed down the road, calling for her to come back again.

After several weeks the Chinese landscape became more and more familiar. Silhouetted against the sky, pagodas turned up their roof corners to ward off descending evil spirits. Endless rice and vegetable fields stretched out to the horizon.

She began to feel at home in the narrow streets swarming with pedestrians, shouting vendors, and jogging coolies balancing their heavy loads on the ends of the poles across their shoulders. Children dodged in and out, as children do in crowds the world over. Older women shuffled by on their bound feet in short, jerky steps; but those younger than middle age were no longer hampered. Nor were there any two-inch fingernails or slant-eyed men sitting in doorways smoking long-stemmed opium pipes. The odor of cooking, animals, and human bodies mingled with an occasional whiff of incense from the open door of a temple.

Buses on the wider streets stopped for passengers to buy boiled sweet potatoes, roasted chestnuts, or sugar cane to chew.

Many shops were built with lumber held together with bamboo pegs. Laborers squatted over rock piles, pounding stones by hand to break up for road surfaces. Once a year, butchers walked in a parade wearing strange little lights hooked into the skin of their foreheads and chests to make sure that they would not be pigs in the next life.

The dragon festival was a gay time for everyone. The mission had two paper dragons. Others had large paper lanterns shaped like fishes, turtles with feet and heads that moved, crabs, grasshoppers; and little boys had front and back halves of paper horses tied around their waists. As they marched, their own legs were the horses' legs, and they appeared to be riding their mounts. Some people carried decorated cardboard shields.

At night the huge dragon came down the street carried by eight men with candles walking under a long, colored cloth. A tongue wagged out of the dragon's mouth at the front. His eyes rolled as though looking around at the crowd. Each of his eight joints moved from side to side. A man ran ahead with a red lantern which the dragon tried to catch but always failed to reach. As the huge beast zig-zagged back and forth, he resembled a great, writing serpent.

The dragon was supposed to frighten away sickness, so everyone rushed out to burn incense and paper money to enlist his protection. The government had tried to break the age-old superstition, but it was deeply rooted. Finally, it was continued with an effort to redirect the enthusiasm into a celebration in support of peace treaties.

"Audience participation" was nothing new in China. Bystanders threw lighted firecrackers at men walking in scanty clothing. Nothing burned their bare bodies as they passed. The falling sparks and waving lanterns were the only light besides the occasional Roman candles shooting into the air.

There were many Chinese customs to startle, often dismay, the newcomer. One day Alice saw a young Chinese girl, little more than a child, ushered into a red chair and carried off on the shoulders of two men. They were followed by a gay party in gala dress.

"What's that all about?" she asked a veteran missionary with her.

"It's a wedding procession," explained her companion. "There has been no courtship. The parents of the young couple have arranged the marriage. No woman, even the bride, attends the wedding ceremony. She does not see her husband until she is taken to him dressed in red like that, carried to her future home in a sedan chair. From then on she belongs to her husband's family and is not supposed to see her girlhood family again."

"But suppose she doesn't like the husband chosen for her?" Alice protested.

"That's just too bad," was the disturbing answer. "She has to make the best of the situation. There is no alternative or escape. She can't run home to mama. She may be utterly miserable, but she has no status until she gives birth to a child, especially a son."

"Suppose the baby's a girl?"

"Unhappily, uneducated people may practice infanticide if the baby is a girl. But this custom is disappearing, even though girls and women are still often considered much like the family livestock."

"If unwanted girls are destroyed in any number, I should think it would bring about an unbalanced adult population," Alice observed.

"Yes, that's correct. There may be a surplus of single adult males."

Alice observed that there seemed to be few middle-aged women. There were little girls, then suddenly only tired, bent, work-worn women who looked old and faded.

A little daughter-in-law had no rights or privileges. She must submit at all times to her husband's mother. The older woman might be unreasonably demanding and impatient with the younger woman's inexperience and lack of skill for her household tasks. Sometimes the mother-in-law was inhumanly cruel. Later, if the daughter-in-law became the older woman in a large household with young daughters-in-law to dominate, she might be like the American college student who suffers hazing in his freshman year. When his turn comes in his sophomore year, he is especially harsh toward the next incoming freshmen.

Many baby girls were given in marriage at birth to a family where a son had also just been born. The girl would grow up with a sense of responsibility for the boy. If the boy died in childhood, the girl was a widow and a slave in her husband's family for life.

A Bible woman told Alice about the grandfather in a family where she had lived. He had made away with his daughters and granddaughters.

Alice shuddered. "But how could they —?"

"A newborn baby girl is just left outside to perish in the elements," was the distressing answer. "It often leaves the few remaining girls and women in the household with back-breaking toil to get all the work done in a large household. But in this family where I lived, the old grandfather became a Christian, and baby girls born since then have been allowed to live."

Many households included several family units and three or four generations under one roof. It took many hands to make a living for so many people. Such large numbers living intimately together were not only unwieldy; they stifled individuality.

These large households often sparked interpersonal tensions. Jealousies and power struggles were inevitable. The wife who had practically no freedom and who must submit to an often tyrannical husband and domineering mother-in-law lived in fear and harbored bitter resentment. With inheritance going to the eldest son, younger sons often felt suppressed hostility. Stress between sexes and between generations was unhappily frequent.

On the other hand, members of the extended family learned to share and to give and take. There were no questions about caring for the aged. Grown sons and daughters took for granted that they were responsible for the welfare of their honored, aging parents and grandparents.

Chengtu experiences were varied and sometimes, unexpected. Alice was awakened one morning by her bed rocking gently. The house squeaked and groaned, and the mosquito netting over the bed swung back and forth. It was her first experience in an earthquake, but it was over in a matter of moments. She had learned what to do in enemy bombing raids; but she decided that there was nothing to be done in the brief seconds of an earthquake, so there was no reason to get excited. With characteristic nonchalance she turned over and went back to sleep.

Along with other foreigners she learned to use substitutes for many items considered to be necessities in her homeland. Because of the prohibitive cost of American soap, she used a little nut that grew on trees. The soft, brown shell made a satisfactory lather and was even effective in washing woolens in the hard Chengtu water.

The day before Christmas found everyone busy. Alice decided to go shopping by herself. She left her bicycle at home. She wanted to look at the stores and people rather than dodge traffic on her bicycle.

To her pleased surprise, the policeman on a corner understood her when she asked the name of a street. Even more surprising, she understood his answer. Even though managing fairly well in the stores, she did not attempt the subtleties of bargaining. She asked prices in different stores, then returned to the shop which had given the best figure.

She wandered into a store which sold beautiful but costly furs. She admired them but purchased nothing. She could find nothing remotely resembling an American dime store, but did see some delightful little wooden toys and silver pins with delicate carvings. After buying some bamboo writing paper, she bargained with a rickshaw puller for the price of a trip back to her residence. She gave him a generous tip and wished him a Merry Christmas. His eyes saucered. Probably he had never heard of Christmas.

On Christmas Eve, she went to the home of Peter Shih and found that she was the only foreigner there. They enjoyed a Chinese feast, some of the food having been raised on the university campus. Before the war, students would not have considered working at such lowly work as farming; but some of the students at the dinner had helped as a part of their regular school program. Student labor proved to be such a financial saving that other schools began to follow the same plan. Madam Chiang-Kai-Shek's dairy herd grazed on the campus lawns, but they were not a part of the school farming.

On Christmas Eve those at the mission made cards and wrapped gifts. Bishop Ward, who was then living in Chengtu, joined when all hung stockings by the fireplace or on the beautiful Christmas tree. The tree had been used for three years. Each time after the celebration, it was put back in the ground until it had grown almost too big — taller than the windows. Some people who had no trees to replant used bamboo poles, tying on branches. Carolers came later in the evening. The first group of about fifteen came from the Methodist church in Chengtu. Afterward, girls dressed in white came from Gin Ling College. They carried lanterns lighted with candles. At about two o'clock, a group of boys from the university chorus came to sing with guitars. After four hours of sleep, carols on a set of bells awakened everybody to enjoy the stockings filled with cookies, oranges, candy, pencils, safety pins, and cheese.

Alice was beginning her life in China in a time of transition. The vast, diversified country, slowly being knit together, was stirring into massive upheaval. Chiang Kai-Shek's government had come to power in the late 1920s and was to last for twenty years. Because of the war with Japan and numerous other problems, including the struggle against Communism, his government was unable to cope with many economic and political difficulties. Gradually, it was to lose its tenuous grip after World War II.

From being a world in itself, China was becoming a nation in a larger world. The vast, unorganized country was like a huge giant slowly rousing from centuries of dozing. As it tried to pull itself together, it was beginning to look about at other lands and people.

Different outlooks on life were beginning to come into focus as Alice became more and more acquainted with the Oriental culture so unlike her own background. Buddhism taught patience and the suppression of desire, considered to be the cause of suffering. Communist ideas, beginning to seep in, disavowed personal freedom and was opposed to any authority but the state. This broke down the strength of the family. Christianity emphasized freedom of choice and personal responsibility.

Buddhist ideas had contributed to daily attitudes. If an open ditch drained sewage down the village street, or if drought brought devastating famine, so be it. Nobody developed ulcers or had a "nervous breakdown." They believed that the frantic drive to change what was undesirable, unhealthy, or uncomfortable caused unnecessary and futile stress.

The world was getting smaller with rapid communication. Improved transportation encouraged people to travel into each other's countries. Ideological conflicts were inevitable. How did Christianity find acceptance for the benefit of people living in an upset world?

Alice's father had said that sound character was basic to the success of all human endeavor. That character, he had taught Alice, was a religious product made up of morality and concern for others. These traits were better weapons than atom bombs or guided missiles. They would undergird the work Alice hoped to do in this great land of intelligent, hard-working people. She was glimpsing a broad view of the vast opportunity to point the way to effective living in Christian brotherhood.

7
Kien Yang Beginnings

After completing her study at the language school, Alice was sent to the church at Kien Yang. It was located fifty miles to the east from Chengtu, and no missionaries had been stationed there before.

After years of training and varied experiences in her homeland, after long months of difficult and dangerous travel, and more than a year of tedious language study, Alice was at last ready for the fulfillment of her single-minded dedication.

It was a red-letter day when she went through the gates of the city of Kien Yang to begin her life's work. Her spirits soared as she made her way to the church property by the city wall which shut out the River Po.

This property had been an inn before being purchased by the Methodist church. Besides a sanctuary, it included living quarters for workers, many of whom went to outlying areas for a variety of mission programs.

This center was called "the church," or at times, "the rural center." Entering from the street, one faced a courtyard bordered by the kitchen and some of the living quarters. Across the courtyard stood the church and beyond the church a second courtyard surrounded by more living quarters.

The "compound" was typically Chinese; the walls

were made of bamboo matting covered with mud plaster. Thin rice paper covered latticed windows. Passersby often wet a finger to moisten the paper and peer inside to see what was going on.

A rope over a six-foot, three-inch frame, all over a "saw horse" and covered with a palm fiber mattress, provided a reasonably comfortable bed. The only light at night was improvised from a candle in a saucer of vegetable oil. The only heat came from a low, flat pan of charcoal. Charcoal was expensive and was used sparingly.

The partitions around Alice's room reached halfway to the ceiling. Light filtered in between the roof tiles. From her room she could hear a service in the sanctuary or her neighbor washing his teeth or snoring at night.

Shops on either side of the property shared common walls with the church. They allowed no privacy. Everything could be heard on either side and the cracks allowed observation of all that a neighbor might be doing.

The District Superintendent lived on the farther side of the sanctuary and, in all, there were sixteen workers at the Center, including the two missionaries just arriving. These workers went out to farmers for agricultural programs, industrial projects, mass educational classes, nursery schools, and mothercraft workshops.

Alice was surprised when even the next-door neighbor did not know where the place of worship was supposed to be. No missionary had lived there before.

Irma Highbaugh, an older, experienced missionary, went to Kien Yang with Alice. Forceful and efficient, she was accustomed to assuming leadership and telling people what to do. Alice had managed her own life, made decisions and shouldered important responsibilities. Living and working together in such close daily contact, made interpersonal stress inevitable. They had not been of each other's choice, were alone thousands of miles from friends and family, foreigners among people whose customs and language were different.

They talked over their relationship and prayed for understanding and patience, then continued to work together effectively. After two busy years, Irma left on her furlough, returning later to another post. Her leadership had been especially significant at the Rural Center.

Although Kien Yang had Buddhist, Taoist, and Confucian temples, they were poorly maintained and were often used for purposes other than worship. Worship was highly individual. The shopper might go into the temple and find a withdrawn worshiper praying quietly before an idol, unconcerned with the noise and bustle of the business being carried on around him.

Priests from the temples wielded considerable power in the community. They promoted festivals and conducted birth, marriage, and burial ceremonies; but they trained no workers and sponsored no welfare programs. Their relations with the Christian church were friendly and cooperative.

Alice had gone to China to show people the meaning of Christian living. She had no thought of opposing established customs or meddling in political affairs. But she sometimes met a wall of unreasonable opposition. Anyone from another country with different customs, different living conditions, and a different religious faith was often subject to suspicion, even hostility.

At first, when children saw an American coming, they would hide in terror. They had been told that these "foreign devils" took out children's eyes to make medicine.

But bit by bit, the program began to get underway. Japanese planes came overhead for frequent bombings, but their aim focused on air fields, and the church work carried on. They began a small industry of embroidery with ten women and later a mothercraft class. The property of a day school, discontinued for lack of leadership, was used for the mothercraft classes. Teachers were trained to instruct mothers in child care and to demonstrate methods of efficient housekeeping and sanitation.

Alice taught English in the Lo Family Flower Garden to help start their school for mass education and a nursery school, then went across the river to the nursery school and mass education class there.

Sweet peas were blooming and the sugar cane was being replanted. Plum and peach blossoms were in flower. Trees were beginning to leaf out and roses to bud. Spring was in the air!

Buffalo grass thickened under ginkgo trees with their veinless leaves growing out of their branches and trunks. In the fall, they would turn a dazzling golden yellow before dropping to cover the ground.

Alice and Irma went out into the country to invite the families to come to the city for the church activities. Conjaho, five miles away, was the first outlying center. Except for the Bible woman there, workers lived at the church in Kien Yang, and walked back and forth to the Conjaho work.

Makeshift was in daily demand. Having no rope, an improvised clothesline was made of bamboo poles. Until a well and pump were available, water for all purposes had to be carried on human backs from a half mile away.

There was no electricity, so Alice, whose skill in devising many kinds of ingenious equipment was needed in a variety of situations, ran her slide projector on an automobile battery. The first time the projector was used, such a large crowd came to see the pictures that they shoved and pushed until the frail walls fell out. For later programs the walls, set with wooden pegs, were removed and set aside beforehand.

Without electricity, Alice also had to operate her radio on an automobile battery. There was only one other radio in all of Kien Yang, a city of 20,000, and it could only reach the Chengtu station fifty miles away.

When she first plugged hers in, music poured out clear and strong. Young people, then older folks, began to gather in excitement to listen. Later they were able to reach several stations: Nanking, Chungking, and, once or twice, a station in India. They heard a CBS newscast by short wave from Honolulu. One night an English broadcast from Chengtu came forth with the aged ditty, "Marizee totes."

It was exciting to hear an occasional San Francisco broadcast. It instantly spanned the distance it had taken Alice four months to cover. But world news was disturbing. Killings, destruction, and chaos were raging over the globe like a forest fire.

The varied church program aimed to work toward a better world and way of life. A Bible woman, Quo Shih Mu, lived in the home of a non-Christian farm family when she first took up her tasks. One of the daughters-in-law had been so unhappy she had hanged herself in the room offered by the grandfather to Quo Shih Mu. He believed that it was full of evil spirits and good enough for the Bible woman. Later, when Alice visited the family, she was invited to stay with Quo Shih Mu. She wondered about those evil spirits when she heard strange sounds closeby in the night. The next morning, she discovered that a water buffalo in the adjoining room had been chewing his cud all night.

A plot of ground was found for Quo Shih Mu, for a

dollar a year for ninety-nine years. It was an abandoned graveyard and supposedly full of evil spirits. The Bible woman organized a team of workers and soon had an adobe house with a red tile roof. Every morning, neighbors asked how many evil spirits she had had to fight off the night before. She could always report that she had slept well.

Hoping to show their intention of cooperating with the government, nurses from the church staff offered to assist with the anti-cholera inoculations. These were announced by a parade through the streets. When Alice was invited to march in the parade, she shouldered her poster and marched with the others. People carried posters explaining what was to be done and commanding cooperation. Such inoculations were given in the city and in the nearby outlying country.

Some of the Chinese workers were invited to take part in the management of the church finances. But the missionaries were like the rider who leads his horse to water but cannot make him drink. Although offering their co-workers the opportunity to assist with the management of church funds, they could not force them to take over the task. Workers of limited ability were willing to rush in to take command, but the more capable refused to assume the responsibility.

The Kien Yang church work began to grow. At last the children, at first afraid of "foreigners," were coming to Sunday School. Old superstitions faded slowly; but gradually, young people and adults were beginning to come to the church activities.

There was so little religious educational material that Alice and Irma decided to write something on parent education, kindergarten methods, and work with primary school children. They wrote in English and found someone to translate the manuscript for printing.

Various questions arose about religious programs. Should the church use candles in the service of worship? The Buddhists did. Could and should they be made to show a difference in meaning? Should they use firecrackers? Was it only a Western idea that firecrackers should not be used, or was there some Christian principle involved? How far should they go in breaking the superstition that only white could be used at funerals? Was an exciting Buddhist or non-Christian funeral with hired mourners, feasts, and firecrackers more comforting than the quiet solemnity of a Christian burial?

One day, Alice stepped out through the church gate in time to see a large funeral procession filling the street. Banners had lined the streets by day, candles by night. She saw the paper replica of the house of the deceased, life-sized paper people, and flags of all shapes and colors with pictures and word characters. Next came fifty children carrying paper banners of various colors, and fifteen men with thirty bushel baskets of paper money. All of these articles would be burned at the grave in order to accompany the deceased into the afterlife. Two men carried three small children dressed in white, wearing white crowns. One child held the ancestral tablet, a small piece of wood draped in black. After this came six or eight silk banners, each worth several hundred dollars. These were followed by a special altar with a picture of the deceased framed with paper flowers. Two older children, also dressed in white, walked beside the picture. A band composed of beggars followed. The casket had led the procession with a live rooster on the top to lead the spirit to Heaven.

The cost of such a ceremony was enormous. It might amount to the total earnings of a couple of months. The price of the banners, paper figures, money, and cloth to be burned at the grave would have been staggering, to say nothing of the wages of so many marchers, the Buddhist priests, and the feast later for relatives.

It presented a startling contrast when, at New Year's, the brother of the church gatekeeper died on the street as an opium beggar. Each worker at the church contributed ten dollars to buy boards for a box, the only cost of his simple, equally non-Christian burial.

Grace Manly had been born and reared in China of missionary parents. For years, she had worked in China, living like the Chinese, and sometimes being taken for Chinese. She lived with a Bible woman and was the only foreigner in the city where she resided. Aliced admired her and wished that she, too, might look like her Chinese co-workers. However, the leopard could not change his spots, she quoted. No matter what she might do, her fair complexion and red-gold hair would forever stand in the way of her looking Chinese.

She was excited when Grace invited her to go on a visit to several churches in the outlying district. They set out together, picking their way along narrow, elevated paths dividing waterfilled rice paddies and fields of other growing produce. Farmers stooped under their conical, wide-brimmed hats to work in their fields. Here and there the workers' houses broke into the landscape.

Alice and Grace walked on and on for eight hours, only stopping now and then to rest. Grace strode along steadily as though wound up by a spring that never ran down. After walking thirty-six miles, she directed a church service at night. Later, when Alice lay in bed exhausted, she heard Grace jumping rope to "keep fit."

The next day Grace took compassion on Alice and ordered a whagger for her. She said that when Alice had spent as many years tramping China's winding paths as she had done, Alice would need no chair, either. But Alice again took pity on the men carrying her and walked much of the way.

On one trip with Grace, the country was unusually hilly. It was covered with bamboo, cedars, tung-oil trees, and a few pines. They walked along narrow paths floored with stones set in place long years before. Each farmer was responsible for maintaining the paths through and beside his land. Many stones had been hollowed out by the thousands of feet that had trod them. When meeting anyone, each traveler had to step off into the rice field or balance precariously on one side to let the other pass.

Small clusters of donkeys or ponies carrying rice or coal traveled along the roads with them. Men were often as heavily loaded as their animals. Sometimes women were the burden bearers. On one trip, a woman carrier shouldered Grace and Alice's bedding and other equipment for two days of their journey.

People inquired everywhere about Grace's mother and father. She was treated like one of their own family. They delighted in telling stories about her father's early visits and the times they had held her as a baby. Grace knew most of the church people everywhere, and introduced Alice to them without hesitating for a name. People came to Grace with personal problems, church problems, or financial troubles. She could talk in a meeting, preach a sermon, tell a story, or sing a song — all in Chinese.

They ate a variety of Chinese food. Breakfast often included pork, fish, liver, stomach, brains, eels and beans, peas, onions, and candied fruit.

For three weeks, they traveled and visited churches. Grace walked the entire distance while Alice walked about eighty miles, most of it on narrow stone paths.

They visited several villages, helped plan church budgets, organized churches and young people's groups, aided teachers in solving school problems, and served as general jacks-of-all-trades.

They visited the rich and the poor. In many of the villages they found people who suffered serious illnesses. Some were dying, but there was no Western medical care or modern medicines for them. Grace picked up undernourished, sickly little children to love and comfort.

Soon after returning at the end of the week, Grace became seriously ill. She was hurried by jeep to Chengtu where her sister was a doctor in the hospital. The cause of her illness was Manchevrian Typhus from the bite of a louse, rare in the province of Szechwan. The infection spread rapidly and, as almost always, it was fatal. Grace died. Although Alice came down with a fever of unknown origin, it gradually disappeared leaving her extremely weak for days.

Grace was buried in the cemetery for foreigners in Chengtu. The brief service was attended by scores of Chinese and foreign friends. Her memory was a guiding light throughout Alice's many later years of dedicated service.

8
Making Do

Many customs and privations from the former life in the United States made it necessary to "make do" with unfamiliar adjustments in life. For example: Alice made all of her clothes. Dress material was purchased by the meter. A length of nine or ten feet of cloth was needed for a dress. She soon set aside the clothes she had brought with her and wore only Chinese garb. She had no difficulty selling some of her former dresses.

Stockings were made with "Chinese feet." Several layers of cloth were sewn into the sole of the stocking. The thick layer was both comfortable and lasting.

Winter cold was especially chilling with limited heating in the houses. Alice wore a padded gown, woolen trousers which she knit from an old skirt, a heavy cloth coat, Chinese shoes, and woolen stockings.

When no rains came and the rice was gone, other vegetables followed, but in short supply. Girls were sometimes sold or given to other families because there was no food for them. A whagger carrier on one of Alice's trips said that he had married off his eleven-year-old daughter because he had no food for her.

Such extreme needs were not only in finances. Superstitions also created impossible situations. In

Kien Yang, a number of houses were burned and others threatened. People feared that the fire god was angry. A local official came to the Kien Yang church asking for a contribution to a fund to hire a Buddhist priest to pray to the fire god. Alice quietly explained that they could not help with that project but they would welcome people who were made homeless by the fire. They could also help people rebuild their houses. The officials thought such an idea was preposterous and they were sure the fire god would attack anyone who helped the unfortunates. Alice explained that Christians prayed to a loving God of all the world. There was no need to be afraid of the fire god. For weeks after this, the non-Christian cook at the church was especially careful with the kitchen fire to be sure the fire god would not take his spite out on them and burn the church property.

One day a neighbor was to receive a new bride. Alice followed the others into the bride's new home. Some went on into her bedroom. The unhappy little bride sat with bowed head on the edge of the bed. She was ill with tuberculosis and had left her bed in her childhood home to make the wedding trip to the house of the groom. Her new in-laws scoffed at foreign medicine and understood nothing of her condition.

Alice was helpless. She knew that the entire family of the groom could become infected with tuberculosis as the pathetic little bride was forced to spend her last days in a house where she did not want to be and with people she did not want to have as a family. The usual firecrackers punctuated the ceremony of taking red pillows, red eggs, new dresses, new quilts, and meat and chicken to the wedding celebration.

Alice felt a renewed determination to be helpful.

She wanted to relieve family misery, rid people of crippling superstition, and make sure that sickly children had the care they needed to become healthy.

Her work varied. She taught English and classes in Bible study. There had been no religious education program in Kien Yang when she first arrived; and before long, she and Irma Highbaugh had organized Sunday Schools in all five rural centers.

Alice had charge of a class for illiterate non-Christian women. Although they were beginning to lose their fear of these "foreign devils," they still held a fixed idea that they could never understand a foreigner; and the foreigner could never understand their customs and ideas. They had little inclination to attempt anything that a foreigner might suggest. Chinese teachers were asked to help.

One day Alice was talking in Chinese to a little Chinese woman. "I didn't know *I* could speak English," the little farm woman said after chatting for some time. She supposed that Alice could only speak English, so they must have been talking in English!

Alice dramatized local situations to illustrate the lectures. One play portrayed the difference between a happy Christian home and an unhappy one with its superstitions. Alice dressed up to play the part of the second daughter-in-law who was jealous of the first daughter-in-law.

Soon after Grace Manley's death, Alice's schedule demanded travel over the entire district. Roads were often bad. Costs were escalating. In Tzechung, she held a meeting on education. It included two districts. She found that Bible women came to her with their problem, as they had gone to Grace. Money for salaries was suddenly her problem. Some elementary schools in Kien Yang were under her supervision, and supplying materials for many Sunday Schools was her job.

Most of what she said in Chinese was now understood. However, the lack of reading and writing skills was a handicap; and she was determined to continue her study. With the additional responsibilities came a new realization of the spiritual strength available to help her conquer seemingly insurmountable obstacles.

A Christian Education Workshop proved to be an outstanding success, although Alice was disappointed not to have accomplished all she had hoped to do. With about sixty adults and half again as many children, there were innumerable problems in explaining Christian motives and ideals. This was done in cooperation with the evangelistic program carried on by the entire church conference.

Delegates to the conference came from four locations. Some were teachers, some farmers, others Bible women and pastors. Some could scarcely read and many had no Bibles. Two teenage boys had come from a farm and had attended school only briefly. All were influential in their communities. It was the first such gathering in the area for study and planning together.

As Alice visited in towns where churches were growing, new members were asked searching questions: When did you become a Christian? Why? Do you have family prayers, and if not, why not? Can you repeat the Lord's Prayer and the Ten Commandments from memory? Do you have a hymn book and a Bible? What do you have in your house to indicate that you are a Christian? Do you burn incense to the ancestors or observe idol worship?

These questions might sound strange, but they were relevant to becoming an intelligent Christian.

Many people attending services at the church, even working on programs, did not call themselves Christians. They were interested, questioning, and impressed as they observed attitudes of Christian tolerance, fair play and, compassion.

A young teacher in the nursery school asked for baptism and showed admirable courage when she stood up before the altar of the church to state her faith. Knowing the almost certain difficulties and possible open disapproval that she would encounter, her Christian belief gave her the strength to stand firm.

Evidence of being a country at war continued to intrude everywhere. On her way to church one Sunday morning, Alice was enjoying the fresh clean air from a rain the night before. Children were wading in the river. Adults were washing their clothes along the banks. People in church wore flowers in their hair. Two old women in tattered rags had picked orchids beside the road for "corsages." But then came the deafening roar of Japanese war planes overhead. Fighting could never be entirely forgotten.

One day, two Japanese airplanes came low over the mission, and suddenly crashed beyond the city wall. One cut a swath through a sugar cane field as it skidded to a halt. The other landed across the river and caught fire, killing the pilot. Many people in Kien Yang had never seen an airplane except in the sky overhead. Mobs quickly swarmed around the two wrecks, asking naive questions. What remained of the planes and the body of the pilot who was killed were quickly carried away. The crowds of unlookers, unhappily, made off with much of the farmer's sugar cane.

It was Alice's responsibility to plan for the fall Christian Education meetings, when the Bishop came to visit the district. The program included workshops and classes in leadership training. The long list of details made her feel, she said, like her father's name for her, Alice in Wonderland. This was the first time

Alice tried to visit the district churches alone after Grace Manley's death.

When Alice returned the thirty miles to Kien Yang, she walked half of the way and rode in a whagger the other fifteen miles. On another trip over the district, Alice walked more than a hundred miles. She also traveled by whagger, truck, and rickshaw. She had seen churches in the last stages of disintegration for lack of financial support. She had also seen churches moving forward. Some were making their first attempts at self-support.

She wrote, "It's hard to realize how utterly new and strange a Christian life is to a person from a Buddhist or Taoist background. People can talk about Chinese philosophers and how they taught what Jesus preached long before the first century, but somehow those things needed the life of Jesus to bring them to life in the acts and thinking of common people. You know how some Christians of America have faith in the bad luck of a black cat. Just imagine a person with only a religion resembling that black cat faith, and how completely new would be the freedom of faith in a loving God, yet how difficult to completely free oneself of the fear of the 'black cat.' Not to burn incense when everyone around predicts terrible results to you and your family because of your faithlessness to your ancestors is frightening."

It was pleasing as Alice visited in Chinese homes to be accepted more and more as a member of the household, instead of a visitor to be pampered. When help was needed for household tasks, she could take over such work as building a fire, sweeping, or cooking. She explained principles of wise, balanced nutrition. She occasionally offered to prepare new, inexpensive dishes. Her American bread was especially appreciated.

On one trip, she crossed the river from Kien Yang

to a little tea house, then climbed a steep hill to a pagoda on a sharp peak. Smoke from a sugar refinery (white sugar) rose into the air. It was the only white sugar being refined in the province of Szechwan. Other refineries processed brown sugar.

Once, Easter services were held in a temple in a Buddhist nunnery. It was unusually clean. The women never married and dressed like the priests. Only their voices marked them as women. Or, a glance downward might show tiny feet that had been bound. Their shaved heads revealed the nine scars burned by incense when they had been initiated.

The idols of this temple were, surprisingly, clean and freshly painted. These Buddhist devotees believed that evil desire was a part of man's nature, and must be accepted and dealt with as best one could. Alice felt a renewed urge to let people know of the Christian hope of a better world ruled by a loving God.

She visited another church where a health nurse, a Bible woman, a minister, and two kindergarten teachers lived in the same compound. A special class for poor, illiterate women, and a newly opened mothercraft class were held in the church. They were having difficulties with financial needs and getting trained teachers. The Bible at this location had come from the Women's Bible School in Tzechung. As Bible women grew older, there was urgent need for newly trained workers to take their places. The mothercraft classes prepared many for training in the seminary.

Alice went to Tien Chiao with a tiny white-haired Bible woman for two weeks. It was thirty miles out into the country over an old stone path. They traveled by whagger. There was no worker there, Bible woman or pastor; but they were hoping to find a minister to serve the community.

Life was not all work and no play. There were

times of relaxation and refreshment. Vacations were enjoyed in the mountains or on unusual trips with visitors.

Alice attended a formal reception for the visiting American ambassador. He was earnest and well informed; but he was only one leader, and the whole world was aflame. How great was the need for wise leadership and sound programs to encourage human beings to get along with one another in Christian brotherhood!

Visiting workers were able to travel by riverboat, and Alice wrote to her Aunt Tee, "The water was smooth and the banks were covered with giant grass about four feet tall, making one feel as if he were looking through a microscope. The big hills stand at a respectable distance, like a ring of children with clasped hands watching us. At other times the hills come close, and the water becomes choppy and full of waves and foam, as we go over rapids buried deep below the water surface. At such times we sail along at an amazing pace until we come onto a shallow stretch and stick on a rock. Then the boatman climbs out, lifts the boat off, and away we go. It is delightful to ride this way for we can read, write, sleep, visit, or stand to watch the view as we wish. We have a bamboo matting cover over the main part of the boat, so we don't mind the rain and the wind isn't too cold.

"The boats going up river are hauled by 'trackers' along the bank. Sometimes a little fishing canoe will come along; and when the rapids become too strong along the shallow bank, the boatman will climb out and pull the boat along behind him. Sometimes one sees a whagger on the old stone road. It looks like a white caterpiller crawling along the bank.

"Our boatman stopped rowing a few minutes to smoke. His pipe is a piece of bamboo with a hole in the end next to the root. In this he puts a pinch of tobacco, took a flint and a piece of paper out of a cup made of bamboo, and lit the paper by striking the flint with a piece of iron. Each pinch of tobacco is good for one puff. After four puffs he put everything away and we went on. This boat is the man's home. He cooks, eats, and sleeps on it. His total possessions seem to be a padded coat, rice for one day, sweet potatoes, wood for one day, an iron kettle and clay stove, a cape of palm fibre for rain, a straw hat, and the boat. The rope to pull the boat upstream is also made of bamboo. The boat itself is made of pine boards."

Alice would have enjoyed fishing when traveling on the river. Unfortunately, all she could have used would have been a bent pin and a bamboo pole.

Fishing in Szechwan was done with an immense net let down into the water from the end of the boat. It took several men to manage it. If a man were fishing alone, he would use a string of hooks on a rope stretched across the river, under the water's surface. He would check his line a couple of times a day. Only very small children used a pole and line. Foreigners might dream of a boat for a "day off," but they usually enjoyed outings in the mountains instead.

One summer in the mountains, on a trip to Yuinshien, Alice's poetic appreciation of beauty appeared when she wrote, "The ferns grow over the rocks like water falling from cliff to cliff, and the trees on the hill opposite are like people seated in a great amphitheater to watch the play in the green valley below. Fields of corn and rice cover the valley floor in orderly rows like choristers ready to join in a great oratorio or pageant.

"We can see Omei, the sacred mountain of West China; and behind it, a big white snow peak from the ranges of Tibet, Minnagonka. This appears at times like a piece of pearl pasted in the sky high above nearer mountain ranges."

Traveling by boat provided scenic grandeur, missed on the man-made road by land. Towering boulders rose like walls on either side of the river. Each fisherman, in his little flatbottomed canoe, had a cormorant to dive for fish. He would drop a bright yellow net with one hand while he guided his boat with a long bamboo pole in the other hand. The boats slipped down over the treacherous rapids with graceful bravado.

Alice often slept on board at night with barely enough room to stretch out full length. The next morning, breakfast might consist of rice, bean curd, meat, and hot green peppers — a typical Szechwan meal.

At the Hartford Seminary, Alice had dreamed and planned with fellow students for work in Tibet. The door to that country had closed; but now she was working where, on a clear day, she could see snowy Tibetan mountains in the distance. She decided to take a trip to Tienti, where it seemed as though she could reach across a narrow valley and touch this land of her first missionary goal.

In Tienti, groves of bamboo trees arched overhead. Masses of roots and hanging moss lined their path. They climbed over boulders and waded through mud. Once the carrier spotted a leopard. Flowers bloomed profusely: buttercups, bluebells, wild roses, and orchids. Wild blackberries grew with generous abandon. Unfamiliar birds and brilliant butterflies flashed in the sunshine.

A large temple on the top of Tienti stood, surprisingly, in a cabbage patch. It was built around a pool in an open court. The pool supplied water from the roof when it rained, and travelers were politely requested not to spit in it. Untidy priests in soiled robes offered gracious hospitality.

Shavings and straw mats covered the wooden beds

in the sleeping quarters. Windows opened to the east on a full moon at night and a morning sun behind banks of clouds covering rugged mountains. A few evergreen trees stood out against the sky like the last memories of an ancient past.

During the day, a priest sat cross-legged before a shrine and chanted prayers. He took no notice of anyone around him. At intervals he rang a bell and shook a rattle decorated with fancy ribbons. He remained at his task until late at night and began again long before dawn. At sunrise, drums accompanied other chanting priests.

It was not clear whether proof of devotion demanded total exhaustion, or whether the worshiper was a practitioner of self-hypnosis. His sincerity offered an impressive example to some from other lands who would rush off from a hasty hour of Sunday worship to follow their everyday pursuits.

In the vacation house on the mountain, only two of the household of guests were from the same mission. Guests had come from the United States, Canada, China, England, and Scotland. Ages ranged from thirty-five to seventy. Yet a spirit of belonging knitted the group together in the realization of their common purpose and the delights of their companionship. They understood their difficult, complicated task.

Although there were few trained leaders, the missionary's job was mostly supervisory. Only Chinese could be named pastors or school principals. Alice worked with Bible women and schools where women were the leaders. An older missionary said, "You new missionaries have a more difficult time than we did. Chinese society has begun to absorb the church as it has absorbed every other culture and religion that ever came to her. Even Jews have been absorbed and lost sight of."

Would the organized Christian church, for

example, be absorbed by the time-honored custom of ancestor worship? Would Western forms of government be lost in the Chinese traditions that traced back to imperial dynasties? Everything everywhere seemed to be changing with dizzying rapidity. Alice wondered how much would change in the firmly established patterns of Chinese life, which had absorbed, rather than been influenced by, other ideas and ways of living?

9
Travel in Szechwan

China continued to be in upheaval. Fear of Japanese bombs, food shortages, runaway inflation with increased taxes, and higher rents stalked the land. Peasants were bitter, and students and university faculty were hostile. Parts of many cities lay in ruins, and ninety percent of the railroad lines had been destroyed. Chiang Kai-Shek seemed unable to cope with the enormous task of shaping a great, diversified mass of people into a great nation.

Among other problems, public transportation was uncertain. Country roads were infested with bandits. Mail trucks were often delayed, and the public bus service disrupted.

Bus overcrowding was illegal; but many would-be passengers waited beyond the city limits to climb aboard already overloaded trucks, hanging on precariously to whatever or whomever was within reach. These illegal passengers were dubbed "yellow fish." Often some urgent need forced Alice to resort to such transportation.

As she traveled about, she became accustomed to personal questions: Where had she come from? Where was she going? How old was she? Why did she have freckles? How much did her dress cost? Where did she get the gold in her teeth? Why was her skin so pale?

Whagger travel was comfortable, but slow. It was like riding in a hammock, and she could have caught up on sleep if there had not been so much of interest to see along the way. Two men carried her chair, another her baggage, and it always arrived with her instead of weeks, or even months, later. Long after her arrival in Kien Yang, she had learned that boxes shipped as she was leaving the States were still in Shanghai waiting, waiting, waiting.

On one of her first trips alone, she stayed at an inn in the back of a tea shop. Her carriers looked after her, even ordering her meals for her. Her room contrasted sharply with the interesting and beautiful scenery she had enjoyed. It had a mud floor and walls that did not reach the ceiling. There were no windows. A small pan with vegetable oil and a tiny wick provided the only light. When undressing for bed, she heard the wife of the innkeeper say, "She's like us!" Alice did not realize that she was having an important initiation into what would involve miles and miles, as well as weeks and weeks, of future travel throughout the province of Szechwan.

Later, as she went about the district, she slept in many other windowless rooms with mud floors and walls. A rural building usually surrounded a court and had a roof of red tile. One room might be occupied by the family pig; pork was an important protein in the Chinese diet. Oxen were also stabled in the house, where they would be out of the cold and safe from thieves. Cackling chickens and snuffling pigs provided familiar sights and sounds. She had never realized how clean pigs could be. They always used one part of the pen for eating and another for defecation. They were never allowed outside the house for exercise because their fat was choice food.

Countless villages dotting the countryside offered no motels or overnight accommodations in their maze of crowded, crooked streets. An occasional opium den broke into the lines of dimly lighted shops. Cries of vendors selling nuts, fruit, and rice cakes mingled with the din of swarming humanity, grunting pigs, and barking dogs. Alice had to sleep wherever she could find a spot to set up her folding cot.

Temples were numerous and always open. People came and went, buying and selling, or eating and sleeping before scowling idols lining the walls. No one objected or even seemed to notice the weary wayfarer.

One stormy night, tired and wet, Alice went with her companion into a temple to get out of a driving rain. No one paid any attention as she opened her folding cot and lay down fully clothed to get some rest. A dark-robed priest with a shaved head disappeared beyond a long row of menacing idols. The boom of a distant gong echoed through the dusty temple.

She fell asleep and was awakened before dawn by the fragrance of incense. She opened her eyes to see a kneeling coolie bowing across her feet before an idol carved in writhing contortions. The worshiper did not stir as she slipped out from under her coat, folded her cot, and quietly took her departure.

One Sunday, Alice visited a nearby church of about one hundred members. Many had been poor farmers who had prospered. They emphasized Christian stewardship, taking first steps toward church self-support. One rich farmer had only recently become interested in the church, but caught the spirit of service. Even though it was a year of lean crops, he had given much of the produce from his farm to help the hungry.

Alice attended a Buddhist service where the people burned quantities of food, cloth, and ornaments. The priest spoke about many gods. He answered questions but there was no program of continuing education for converts. They were left to grope and flounder, as had their ancestors for years gone by.

The priest in the temple was friendly, clearly complimented by the attendance and interest of his foreign visitor. Alice was thoughtful. Buddhism had lasted for hundreds of years. Did it rest on consecration, on the abandonment of self, she wondered? Christianity transformed lives, and she realized anew that God was willing to work in the lives of all people.

One time Alice was to attend an annual conference in Chungking. Her transportation difficulties were typical of many trips. She waited all day for an alcohol truck. The driver had offered to take her, but he later decided not to go. The next day she went to the public bus station and waited. Finally, she had an opportunity to go on a bus, but for twice the usual fare.

That night the bus reached Neikiang, and the next morning she was unable to get another bus to take her on to Chungking. Finally, along came a military truck crowded with "yellow fish." Among them was a missionary friend who had a special pass. He took Alice as a co-worker. He belonged to an organization called "Friends of Transient Soldiers" with designated stops in churches along the road. When the truck came to towns where there would be an inspection, the other passengers would have to get off, walk a mile or two around the town, and get on again beyond the city limits. Alice enjoyed the privilege of staying on the truck instead of walking, carrying her eighty pounds of baggage.

When she found a fellow missionary along the way bound for the same meetings in Chungking, Alice begged a place for her to squeeze into the overloaded truck. When they were going through baggage and passport inspection at Pishan, it was discovered that the driver had not reported the correct number of passengers and was fined for carrying "yellow fish." All passengers had to find another truck. Alice and her friend waited for several hours. They were happy when an army officer came along and said that since they were guests of his country, he would help them get a ride into Chungking. They saw their precious truck driver wink, climb into his truck, and drive off. Calling a baggage carrier, they hurried after him. After dog-trotting for about a mile, they found him sitting peacefully by the road waiting for his passengers.

All climbed into the truck again. After negotiating hairpin curves and steep roads, over mountains and through a tunnel, the truck's engine suddenly began to cough and sputter. Everyone jumped out to haul, pull, and push, then climb aboard again to ride a few miles before a motorcycle appeared. The rider had news that Chiang Kai-Shek was coming. Hurriedly, everyone climbed off the slowly moving truck. Of course, the Generalissimo couldn't guess why about forty people were left stranded with baggage in the country! Apparently, he was uninterested in illegal "yellow fish" as he drove on by. The passengers were left to get into Chungking any way they could find.

Alice and her fellow missionary traveler were still hoping to get to the meetings in Chungking, but their prospects began to fade. Then a soldier happened along in another truck. He took their baggage to the nearest town where they caught up with it on foot and bought tickets to continue by horse cart. A tiny horse, about the size of a Shetland pony, pulled five people in an open two-wheeled cart. Finally, they arrived in Chungking for the evening sessions, instead of the opening noon meeting.

Alice felt uncomfortably disheveled. Electric lights glared down mercilessly. Vast throngs of people rushed here and there. Cars and buses whizzed by with honking horns. American jeeps bearing United States insignia scuttled through the crowded streets. They walked for what seemed like miles without leaving the inner section of the huge city. Alice mentally had to leave the small villages behind her for this great city of over a million people.

The Chungking Annual Conference was well attended. The year before, only three "foreigners" had been present. Now there were twenty-seven. Many young people were asking to study at the seminary. Reports indicated that several points in the district were moving toward self-support.

On one trip, Alice and a young Chinese girl took turns waiting by the road for a truck to take them to the next town. Three Chinese officers, who had been studying English with Alice at the church, summoned whaggers for them and paid the carriers to take them to a place where they would be able to get rickshaws.

The Chinese servicemen she saw often seemed to know little about the war. Japanese air raids continued, but it was difficult to know which way the fighting was going. Alice slept through the bombing untroubled; but she was distressed by what was happening to many people, both in the air and on the ground.

When an American plane crashed near Kien Yang, no one was injured, fortunately. Alice met the men who came to repair the plane and found them delighted to be able to talk English to someone. Local residents felt honored to have such visitors. When a plane crashed in Suining, people clapped and sent off firecrackers to honor them.

When on a trip to Tzechung, many bridges were out; and travelers had to wade in the icy mountain current up to their waists. Alice thought it a lark. Later she rode in an American army truck. It was a treat to have a place to sit instead of standing in an overcrowded bus or truck subject to frequent breakdowns.

On another trip, Alice was waiting by the road, hoping for bus or truck transportation, when she saw a line of American jeeps coming toward her. It was the first time she had seen her own uniformed countrymen in China. Their open, friendly grins and robust good humor stirred a warm glow. She felt a wave of sudden homesickness.

They stopped and she met Americans from Kansas, Nebraska, and other home states. Although strangers, they all felt a joyous kinship. They chatted about everything from ice cream cones and baseball scores to God and His purpose in a topsy-turvy world.

Sometimes on her trips, Alice would meet a truck of the Friends' Ambulance Service. It provided one of the few bright spots due to war conditions. It was staffed by conscientious objectors from America, some from England, and a few from China. They had all chosen their task and worked without salary, receiving only enough for food and lodging. They encountered all the hardships and hazards of work in a foreign country at war. They had no opportunity to study the language. They traveled two by two, unarmed, with only a Chinese mechanic, who usually knew little English.

These ambulance trucks drove many miles, targets of Japanese snipers. They carried large amounts of medical supplies. If would-be passengers asked for a ride, they had to sign a statement saying that they would not hold the organization responsible in the event of an accident or hold-up.

At night, the men often had to sleep under the truck to guard it and its contents from thieves. They

ALICE LUCILE WEED

The two-story, white frame house in **Rye, Colorado**, where Alice Weed was born.

The church at **Kun Yang**. Pastor Chung, **the Chinese** pastor, is in the pulpit.

The Kien Yang Mothercraft School in 1950.

The Methodist church in Chengdu.

Alice Weed on her baggage-laden motorcycle after a forty-eight mile trip to Chengtu in 1948.

The morning roll call at the Rural Center at Kang Chia Ho.

The Youth Conference on the Mission Farm in Villa Quasada, Costa Rica.

Alice Weed (far left) with students from the Training School for Christian Workers in Alajuela, Costa Rica.

might be on a trip of several days without seeing a bed. In all kinds of weather and under all types of difficulties they never complained. Only a few were hurt or lost their lives due to illness, injury, or gunfire. The Kien Yang church was one of their regular overnight stopping places. These Friends' trucks later were the last to leave Burma with loads of refugees.

There were few times, if any, in Alice's life when she was not mothering somebody. She had noticed a little beggar hobbling down the street in one of her visits to another church. He had only one leg and braced himself with a stick which served as a crude crutch. He was dirty, ragged, and hungry.

Alice learned that he had lost his leg in a bombing raid in a distant city. Taken to a public health hospital, he had been released when the stump healed, but could not find any of his family. It was not clear how he had made his way to Kien Yang; but here he was, only eleven years old, homeless, struggling to keep alive with whatever he could beg.

With characteristic nurturance, Alice took him in, scrubbed him and fed him. He put his begging bowl, carried by such waifs, outside the church gate, and that night several little children came to take it.

His name was Bi Fu San. No one could have predicted, even wildly guessed, how he would develop in the years ahead.

10
India

The end of her first five-year term in China was fast approaching. Alice began to make plans for her work to be carried on while she was on her furlough in the United States. Among other details, she arranged for the little beggar, Bi Fu San, to be left in the care of a Buddhist trade school.

Unsettling rumors continued to spread: The Japanese were coming. They had taken over the country along the coast and were moving farther and farther inland toward the remote western province of Szechwan. The United States did not order the missionaries out of the country, but disclaimed responsibility if they chose to remain in China. The Mission Board pledged its approval of whatever the decision of the missionaries might be.

"Why would you leave the work you have felt called to do?" asked Alice's Chinese co-workers. "We must remain, even if you run away."

The Japanese had pushed Chiang Kai-Shek westward, where he set up his nationalist government in Chungking. Pressures from the western allies and internal economic war needs added to the weakening of his nationalist government.

Alice was approaching the end of five years in

China. It was time for her furlough. Fearful of Japanese paratroopers dropping on the city of Tsechung, Alice and other missionaries slipped away early one morning before dawn to begin the long journey back to the States.

In Chengtu, Alice and Margaret Seek, another missionary, took the first available plane to Kuiming. It was Alice's first plane ride, and the plane was an army convoy with bucket seats along the sides. When she arrived in Kuiming, the American consul who had earlier advised her to leave China exclaimed, "This time you're not getting away with it!"

From Kuiming they flew over the Hump, the highest mountain in the world. When they saw another plane, they never knew whether it was friend or foe.

Each passenger was allowed only twenty-four pounds of luggage. Word had come that they would have no heat. Alice put on thirty-three pounds of clothing, beginning with summer clothes for India. She filled her pockets until they bulged like great tumors. Instead of no heat, they could not turn off the plane's heater.

The snow seemed to be close enough to reach out and make a snowball. As they flew west, the sun set in a fiery ball behind crimson and gold clouds. Two days before, four cargo planes had been lost in a violent storm, but Alice knew that the passenger planes were piloted by some of the best flyers in the world.

Alice was met in Calcutta by people from the China Inland Mission. They represented a newly organized group from all missions to care for people evacuating from China. Their hospitality provided the luxuries of fresh milk, butter, and ice cream. Alice even enjoyed ice cream for breakfast.

More than ninety missionaries arrived from China

in the few days Alice was in Calcutta. They represented all types of missions and many nations. The Bengal government had given buildings, trucks, and bedding for their use. Before the committee to help the refugees was formed, they had had to find their own missions, or some other place to stay in a strange city where they had no acquaintance with the language or the people. Mission stations everywhere were overcrowded with people sleeping on the floor while the local missionaries tried to carry on their regular work.

Alice and Margaret Seek went to the Methodist Lee Memorial School. Calcutta streets swarmed with double-decker buses and horse-drawn carriages with their drivers sitting on a high seat above the passengers. There were bicycles, rickshaws for two, and taxis driven by Sikhs wearing bright-colored turbans over their long hair and beards. White sacred cows wandered at will through the whirling, clamoring mass.

At the Lee Memorial Mission, Alice slept in a room with four others. They ate in the crowded dining room with some thirty other refugee missionaries going through Calcutta.

Alice visited points of interest in Calcutta, and was impressed by the splendor of the Jain Temple and Mohammedan Mosque. They were better cared for than the Buddhist and Taoist temples she had seen in China. The Jain temple to the monkey god glittered with jewels, glass, silver, and gold. Diamonds and rubies glistened in the glare of electric lights. Visitors removed their shoes at the foot of the steps of white marble and walked over inlaid designs on the floor, or looked in mirrors that reflected seven times.

Although there were food rationing, soldiers on the streets, and shortages of many commodities, there were few other evidences of war. She observed some contrasts between India and China. The subtle, firmly entrenched caste system was depressing; in China, the lowliest coolie could become president if he had the ability and opportunity. In India, religions seemed to be distinct from each other. The followers were more separated than in China, where there was a mingling of beliefs and customs. Chinese people seemed to be able to take advantage of Buddhism, Confucianism, and Taoism. They might even include Christianity. It was a matter of culture rather than religion.

After a busy four days in Calcutta, Alice and Margaret Seek took a taxi to the railroad station. The taxi was driven by a huge Sikh with an orange-colored turban. At the station, a wiry little man grabbed her suitcase and (steamer) rug container, hoisted them to the top of his head, and walked off with the command, "Come!" They were soon settled in a compartment with three other passengers.

When they came to the Ganges River, hundreds of people lined the banks, and clusters were bathing where the dead were burned.

No one in their train compartment had any bedding, so they all snuggled down in the winter clothes they had worn out of China. They slept soundly until tea and toast were brought the next morning. As they looked out of the train window, they saw a dry, barren land unlike the green landscape of Szechwan. The yellow soil was badly eroded. Red-headed cranes with white feathers stared as the train sped past. A handsome green parrot or an occasional blue jay appeared against the sky. Camels rocked along the dusty roads with their noses in the air, like haughty royalty. Bullock carts surrounded by clouds of dust plodded along rutted roads. The scattered villages looked much like China, but the people were dressed in bright colors contrasting with the uniform blue of the Chinese.

When they reached Lucknow, six hundred miles from Calcutta, Alice and Margaret took a quaint little two-wheeled cart to the famous Isabella Thoburn College. Its serene quiet and beauty seemed to deny the existence of war and threatening bombs.

Alice visited schools, churches, and agricultural missions across India. She found New Delhi, the eighth city to be built on the ruins of previous cities, to be a spacious, modern city with wide boulevards, verdant parks, and handsome government buildings. She said she felt as though she were walking through the pages of a huge history book showing pictures of palaces and ruins of past glories. She visited the Methodist primary school and other mission work.

In Agra, she saw the primary and industrial mission schools and admired the beautiful rugs students were making. The Taj Mahal was more beautiful than any romantic description Alice had read. She saw it by moonlight and again on a sunny day. When visiting Baroda's mission hospital, school, and seminary, she enjoyed an elephant ride.

In Muttra, the mission schools were surrounded by the famous Hindu centers of worship. At Brindaban, "the playground of Krishna," Alice saw hundreds of temples with temple "widows," or prostitutes. Because they were widows, they were sternly rejected and led a miserable life with the one hope of heaven from serving in the temple.

The pastor of a Christian church had been the head of a large Hindu temple before he had become a Christian.

From Muttra, Alice went out into the country for a week of visiting in churches and schools. She found an opportunity to encourage a fellowship between China's and India's farm Christians. One rural India church began an exchange of letters with a Chinese rural church, sharing mutual problems and reporting successes.

On the Congregational farm near Ahmednagar, Alice taught English briefly in a boys' school. She visited the hospital and nearby villages and attended a Christian farmers institute. Hundreds of village people, mostly farmers, gathered to sing and hear an inspirational message. After each hymn, everyone would raise his hand above his head and shout, "Praise be to Christ! Rah!" More than a thousand sat on the ground to enjoy their picnic meal of wheat cooked with butter and sorghum sugar. People ate with their fingers off banana leaf "plates."

On a trip into the hills, Alice saw Gandhi and was impressed by his simplicity.

India missionaries were generous with their time and energies. As Alice visited and observed, she became better acquainted with the problems of caste, poverty, ignorance, and religious fanaticism. China's problems seemed to be but a part of the world-wide turmoil where hatred, greed, and needless cruelties cried out for Christian brotherhood.

When Alice reached Bombay, she waited with thirty other refugees for transportation to the United States. They stayed at the Methodist Women's Home where the remarkable director, Miss Mildred Drescher, kept everyone happy, well fed, and healthy. They visited churches and other mission work, and helped in the several canteens for soldiers stationed in the city.

No one dared leave the city for any distance or length of time. War had upset all regular schedules of travel. Everyone was on a stand-by list for sudden notice of available transportation. Weekly reports had to be made to the Bombay police.

Alice had broken her glasses weeks before and learned that she could have them replaced while in

Bombay. After a considerable delay, it was a relief to be able to read comfortably again. She took her turn at the busy sewing machines where many guests were replacing their worn, nearly threadbare clothes.

Bombay staged a joyous V-Day celebration on August 16, 1945. Lights appeared on tall buildings for the first time in years. News from China was scanty and undependable, but the possiblity of getting transportation to the States seemed more promising.

At last, the *S. S. Gripsolm* arrived with its overload of China refugees. Altogether, Alice had spent six months in India, three of them waiting in Bombay. However, she had had the opportunity to meet many important Indian leaders and had learned that some of the former "outcasts" were coming into positions of importance.

When Alice went on board the *Gripsholm*, she found so many Chinese friends among the six hundred missionaries that she wondered who had been left in China. Altogether, 1500 people were on board, sleeping on deck and anywhere else where there was room to lie down. No one was allowed ashore at any port; but from the deck it was possible to see the Red Sea, the Suez Canal, and a port in Greece near Athens where three hundred people came on board.

As the ship came into New York harbor, there was a band playing at the foot of the Statue of Liberty. Not a dry eye was to be seen as everyone realized that at last they were HOME in the U.S.A.

Everywhere there were forms to fill out. Alice stood in line for thirteen hours for New York customs inspection. The Red Cross gave out milk, hot coffee, and cookies and helped with baggage and transportation to hotels.

She was soon on her way to Nebraska and Aunt Tee. It was a joy beyond words to be back in her homeland. She had been living where there was no television, radio, or daily English newspaper to keep an American abreast of what was going on in the world at large.

She found that disturbing changes were taking place in her homeland. Different attitudes were pervading college campuses, seeping into labor organizations and altering political causes. Changing economic conditions, social structures, and moral values were confusing. Some were sound, some questionable.

She had come to love China and the Chinese. Was she becoming a "man without a country?" Or, was she moving toward the sympathetic, broader understanding of world citizenship?

11
Return to Kien Yang

The year at the Hartford Seminary gave renewed energies for Alice's return to China. The personnel of the campus had changed; but the same helpful, friendly spirit she had known before remained. She received her Bachelor of Divinity degree but waited to be ordained in China.

A long-cherished hope was fulfilled when she bought a motorscooter. The girls in the seminary dormitory dubbed it "Sally," standing for, they explained, *salvation*, because it "jolted hell out of anyone riding it." Alice took it out for a trial run and found that it provided practical, but in no way luxurious, transportation. Sally would be a definite asset in traveling about over the province of Szechwan.

When she left, taking Aunt Tee with her for the return to China, Alice was given a canner, a pressure cooker, a camera, a projector with good slides, and other articles of immeasurable value for her work in far-off western China.

When they arrived in Shanghai aboard an unconverted troop transport, the *S.S. Marine Lynx*, there was great rejoicing. Both American and Chinese friends in Nanking also greeted her enthusiastically. One little Chinese girl cried as she tried to recount all that Alice had done for her and the people where she had worked. While in Shanghai, every day brought callers who came to welcome her back. One young woman said, "Alice says we are co-workers with her. Few others have told us that."

She was able, after seven years, to retrieve the baggage she had had to leave there when on her way to her first term in far western China. It was undisturbed except for a strange suit of men's clothes on top of everything in her trunk.

World War II was over and the Japanese were gone. Travel lanes were open from Shanghai to the west, and Aunt Tee took the more rapid, comfortable trip from Shanghai to Chengtu by plane, while Alice went by boat up the Yangtse River with the baggage and two Mennonite missionaries.

Alice wrote: "Our boat (from Shanghai) was crowded to the utmost. There wasn't even room to walk on the decks. There were eight of us foreigners. Although I had a whole room to myself, one of the other ladies had a room with three men, so she asked to share my room for dressing. Finally, I slept on the floor outside the cabin or in the dining room along with other Chinese passengers in order to let her have a bed where she could rest. I slept like a log even when officials came in the dining room where I was sleeping and all but stepped on my nose. When we stopped at night because of Communist troubles, we often had to start again very early in the morning, and in that case police came on the boat to examine the passengers and put off any Communist suspects. They always had to have a feast in the room where I was sleeping. We ate Chinese food all the time we were on the boat. Even so, it was cleaner than the American *Marine Lynx*.

"One of the passengers was an old timer who had been in the salt business for thirty some years. He was a very loyal Britisher. One passenger was from Canada and had been in China a year with the

Canadian Aid to China. She could speak no Chinese. One passenger was the principal of the School for missionaries' children in Chengtu. Another was a minister on his second term of service in China. There was also a young Mennonite couple going to Szechwan for the first time to start new work for their mission. At first, we had difficulty finding a place to see, because baggage was piled so high outside our windows. We finally climbed on top of the boat next to the smokestack, and kept well to the center of the roof so we wouldn't fall off when the boat rolled a little. Only the first class had a special place to eat. Everyone else ate where they were sitting when the food was brought on huge trays.

"The landscape was constantly changing. Near Shanghai, the land was flat and filled with little canals that had little sailboats on them. Often it looked as if the boats were gliding along on the ground. At times, the river seemed to be wide and, at other times, it was very narrow with high clay and loam banks on each side. Often, the banks would have great chunks of the field in the water with crops still on them where the river had washed away the bank. Once we ran on a sandbar and had to send out a rowboart to find the river channel again. We met all kinds of river junks, with and without beautiful sails, and also wartime landing craft that had been turned into freight boats. Finally, we came to a huge mountain that seemed to block our pathway and from then on we were in the famous gorges for two days with every minute one of intense interest. OFten in the mountains cliffs towered above us for thousands of feet on each side and there were trails cut in the banks of solid rock for the men who pull the boats up the river. Above us we could see the sunlight making the coloring on the rocks most fascinating. As we progressed, the pilot never let his eyes move from the path of the boat. He never turned his head, but his eyes seemed to be constantly moving. He directed the helmsman by the movement of his fingers, for the roar of the rapids often drowned out one's voice. Sometimes the boat stood still. As the engine strained against the current, the passengers held their breath as the great whirlpools tugged at the boat and drew it slowly toward the bank. Just in time, the boat would lunge forward and float freely but slowly up the river."

Arriving in Kien Yang, Alice and her aunt were the only foreigners in all of the city. The nearest American was fifty miles away in Chengtu. Alice now had the responsibility of supervising the work of the entire rural center. The work of evangelism, education, agricultural aid, industry, and health improvement continued in the five centers located within a five-mile radius of Kien Yang.

A minister and Bible woman directed the work of evangelism. Seminary students doing practice work assisted. There was also a Bible woman living in nearby Conjaho, with a high school graduate practice teaching in the elementary school, another local girl learning to work with nursery school children, and a midwife, who visited in homes and held a clinic in the city and in the rural centers. The District Superintendent and agricultural specialists also lived at the church with the pastor and Alice.

The nursery schools cared for young children. The agricultural centers introduced better seed and improved methods of cultivation. Sugar was raised and refined on the farms around Conjaho. Human labor was replaced by sturdy oxen for work so heavy the animals had to be rested every hour. The industrial center taught hand crafts and textile dyeing.

Alice, in general charge, worked with all, helping to plan programs for different ages, organizing Sunday Schools, and teaching teachers to teach.

She wrote her father about China farming. She wished for good alfalfa seed and a good horse-drawn plow. The Chinese farmers were using a shallow plow; but some of the fields on the river bottom were large enough, Alice estimated, to use a two-furrow plow. She also wished for a cultivator and planter. It was "so wet that listing wouldn't work but check-row would," revealing her girlhood acquaintance with middle west farming in the United States.

One day, after a meeting in the Lo Family Flower Garden farm center, Alice and one of the young girls prepared a plot of ground at the Agricultural Extension Agency. They offered assistance with a crop. Before long another church member appeared, followed by the visiting evangelist. The four workers prepared more than half the field. It was soon ready for planting peas, beans, and wheat. Before leaving on furlough, Alice had introduced tomatoes to the Agricultural Extension Agency. Now they were on the market.

Alice was discovering how interesting and difficult human beings may be. A volunteer worker at the Kien Yang mission lived in the church property for some time. He said that God had not told him to leave, so he would stay. His co-workers in the agricultural agency, he claimed, resented his new faith and his efforts to convert them, so he wished to leave them to God's punishment. Alice labored long and earnestly to open his eyes to his responsibility for doing his own work without being judgmental of others and also to accept the difference between his own wishes and God's will.

The schedule became increasingly heavy. Alice spent two days a week with the new school across the river from Kien Yang. She also taught an English class, directed a children's group in the Sunday School, and worked with both adults as well as children in the general program of the church.

In addition, she had the management of the large mission household of sixteen workers. It involved property maintenance, and such chores as dismissing the old gateman for stealing and finding a new one. Supervising food shopping and meal planning called for daily attention, and the floors and other wood work had to be thoroughly oiled regularly to get rid of persistent bedbugs.

Rats and fleas presented another problem. Cats were prized. Rats carried a disease that often killed them, so they were few. Alice acquired a large yellow cat who set about the reduction of the rat population. He had some typical feline nocturnal habits that caused considerable anxiety one night when he failed to return to the home base the next morning. However, he eventually appeared. Visitors were on hand when he walked in proudly bearing the mangled remains of his nighttime foray. A pet dog was slower to take up his responsibilities, but eventually he grasped the idea that his life's work was to guard the property and personnel from prowlers and thieves.

The cook for Alice and Aunt Tee was a small-boned, thin little man. He was jolly and knowledgeable about American cooking. He always wore an aged felt hat of unknown history. It rested firmly down over his ears. If anything should happen to his treasured headgear, Alice wondered, what sort of nourishment might emerge from his pots and pans? The Chinese co-workers had a different cook.

The kitchen stove was constructed of mud and stones. The oven was made of old gasoline tins. It was the wonder of the countryside. People from farms and from the street came on special tours of inspection to see the stove with an oven and the heating stove with a stovepipe. They asked where the fire was in the heating stove and were amazed at the pipe. The tinsmith had to be told how to make the pipe and the damper, and the neighbors asked what "that thing coming out of the top of the house was." The people understood chimneys of mud and stone in sugar factories, or mud stoves in the kitchen, but nothing like a metal pipe.

Only the church in Chengtu had glass in the windows. In Kien Yang, lattice work on the front window matched the rest of the church buildings. The rice paper kept out the cold when there was no heat or sun.

While Aunt Tee was with her, Alice was able to slip away for a vacation trip to the mountains. She wanted Aunt Tee to see the high blue Tibetan range. At sunset, Minnagona's tip shone bright pink, and Omei, the sacred mountain, seemed close but, in fact, was one hundred miles away.

The journey into the cool altitude led up over high mountains and through little villages like mushrooms clinging to the side of a tree trunk. Aunt Tee declared that she had never worked so hard holding on as she did to her whagger on the steep path.

On the way, about twenty bandits suddenly appeared carrying guns of all kinds of vintages. Aunt Tee was sure one was like a gun her father had had; it was lighted with a match. Some were modern machine guns, some were rifles, but most were antiques. Although the bandits had real bullets, there was no indication of hostility. One man even had a hydrangia protruding from the end of his gun.

Aunt Tee could speak no Chinese, but she managed to communicate with amazing ingenuity with the home cook and members of the church.

The first Annual Conference after their arrival in Kien Yang was a milestone. Alice, another missionary, and two Chinese were the first women to be ordained as deacons in Szechwan.

The Japanese had gone, Chang-Kai-Shek's control was tenuous, and new rumors were spreading about a Communist take-over. After a year with Alice, it seemed best for Aunt Tee to return to the safety of the United States.

An orphanage was opening on Yellow Mountain near Chungking. The land had been given to the Methodist Mission by the Generalissimo and Madame Chiang Kai-Shek. They hoped to care for several hundred homeless children. Alice had been suggested as a worker there, but her work was in Kien Yang.

For a time Alice was alone. Then a slim brunette in her late twenties came from the language school in Peking. It was Jean Rowland's first term as a missionary, and she and Alice together were to experience the harrowing, even dangerous, events ahead.

The two missionaries worked harmoniously to develop the mothercraft classes, the kindergarten program, various projects of the rural center, and other activities. As with Irma Highbaugh, they were miles from the companionship of other Americans. They shared not only mission responsibilities, but home permanent waves and other specialties of personal interest to American women.

As they went about the crowded schedule, more and more signs of serious trouble were evident. They began to sense subtle differences in the attitudes of those about them. On her return, Alice had found that Bi Fu San was miserable in the Buddhist "school," which turned out to be a route to cheap child labor for a local industry. She took him back to the Kien Yang mission and got him a wooden leg, but he was often sullen and uncommunicative.

Problems came from questions of responsibility. Chinese workers had held back from leadership in earlier days. The mission work had been planned, organized, supported, and directed by Americans. Missionaries like Alice had been assigned to initiate and direct what they had been trained to do.

Now Alice found that more and more of the work was being carried by the Chinese themselves. They were taking over without her, convinced of their own abilities and sometimes influenced by disturbing new ideas. It was becoming their own Chinese work in their own land among their own people.

In step with the worldwide emergence of nationalism, the American church abroad was becoming indigenous. As people in foreign countries were demanding political autonomy, churches were moving to take over their own programs. They were growing up. Like the adolescent, they were demanding the opportunity to make their own decisions and run their own affairs. The "home church," like the human parent, faced the need to step back, let the responsibility fall on new shoulders, and carry on only as "helpers," not managers.

Alice sometimes felt left out when Chinese workers went ahead with programs without asking for advice or even reporting what they were doing. How could she be effective without telling inexperienced workers what to do?

"It is amazing," she commented later with characteristic insight and good humor. "The Lord is willing to struggle with us and our shortness of wisdom. I have fallen into the same pit over and over again, forgetting that the vineyard we planted is the Lord's. We have been only husbandmen, not owners."

Flexibility like hers in adjusting to a different organization was essential, as it was essential to the success of other modern missions the world over. The church at Antioch did not tell the people of Corinth what to do. Paul and Silas went to help but did not direct all the work themselves.

Changes were creeping into life all around them. Vague threats of dangerous attacks were spreading, and rumors of military plans were confusing. Alice and Jean made every effort to avoid any remark, gesture, or action that might offend. As they went about life as usual, their calm serenity bolstered the courage of the frightened people around them.

Chinese observers were puzzled. They knew that these two American women could not know what might lie ahead. Could their serenity testify to their faith in a God they trusted to guide and care for them? With no guns, political powers, or consulate to protect them, they were relaxed and cheerful. They even showed a concern for the sly people among them when they later proved to be traitors.

Alice and Jean were troubled by the different living standards of the Chinese and American missionaries. The Chinese had been accustomed to their way of life for generations. People from other countries had no immunity to diseases, as did those born and reared in the country. It could be disastrous for newcomers to eat and live as the natives did.

Yet Alice and Jean were determined to demonstrate that they felt no superiority over the Chinese with whom they worked. They dressed like them, ate the same kind of food, and, if there was need for health care, made sure that their Chinese co-workers had access to the same medications. They had gone to China to help people to know the meaning of Christian love. They had no thought of being disloyal to the government in the country where they had chosen to live and work.

However, this effort to show that they, as Americans, had no advantages not enjoyed by their Chinese co-workers made little impression. Many unschooled, later brain-washed, people refused to accept any concept of foreigners different from their preconceived ideas.

The work of the church, however, moved along busily. The Easter program was a success, with a Good Friday service and a dramatic presentation on Easter Sunday morning. Christmas and New Year's came and went with the usual feasts and other church activities. Outsiders attempted to disrupt one of the programs, a child was trampled and windows broken. But the program continued.

The young people of the church were enthusiastic. A dozen came every morning for early prayer, often regardless of bad weather. The community of Conjaho, in the country with the God's-acre plan, built their own church and organized a school with two teachers. One of the teachers planned to go to the seminary later. Another farm community near the city built a new high school and asked for Christian work there. Yet another community, where Alice had started work during her first term, wanted to build a church; but there was no full-time worker available. A young man, from still another community with opening work, decided to attend the seminary. The young man had had training in the United States Air Force. His family was not Christian and refused to help him financially; but when Alice visited them, they were friendly and more interested.

Alice had brought her new slides on the return from her furlough. Some students had a small army engine to generate current, and for three days they showed the slides for two hours in the afternoon and two hours in the evening, as well as three times on Sunday.

Crowds came by the hundreds; but didn't break anything, as they had first done when Alice had turned on her battery-powered radio. When the first program began, the motor refused to run dependably. The boys knew nothing about motor mechanics and had to ask Alice for help. With her assistance, one of the boys, who had been with the Chinese army in an American training camp, took over.

Finally, the community was soon to have electricity. Without a meter, the cost was to be determined by the number of light bulbs used. A flat monthly rate was charged regardless of how often the light was turned on. It was a relief from the oil lamps used with occasional candles in the past.

Alice's motorscooter, Sally, had been crated in the United States and shipped to her in China. She had asked that a battery be packed with it to use with her slide projector. Unfortunately, the battery leaked onto the scooter in transit. When it arrived in Kien Yang, Alice, with her usual mechanic's skill, took the scooter apart and cleaned it, then put it back together in good running order.

Sally was sometimes out of order because of a broken part. It took so long to get a replacement from Hong Kong that Sally often remained in the Chengtu repair shop. At other times, broken parts were replaced by inventions made under Alice's supervision in a local machine shop.

Much later, when Alice was away and Sally was left with a missionary in Chengtu, the police demanded an exorbitant fee for its possession, then came later and confiscated it, saying that the mission "had no business owning one."

The national officer in charge of the army camp in Kien Yang invited the pastor and Bible woman to come every week to teach games and songs to his soldiers. When new troops arrived, the invitation was repeated because there had been few discipline problems, and no soldier had tried to run away when the mission visitors came. New officers were not Christian, but they recognized the value of what the church workers did for their camp.

Alice's English class met four times a week and included several soldiers. It was mostly a Bible class. When she asked them to choose their subject, they selected the Gospel of Mark. The class included an army doctor, a colonel just returned from India, a dean of students in the girls' high school nearby, a banker, a telegraph operator, a student preparing to enter college in the fall, a customs officer, an insurance man, and a sugar merchant. Others came to listen. The small fee merely covered the cost of the candles or vegetable oil lamps.

Alice worried about widespread malnutrition. Trying to meet the needs was like trying to empty the ocean with a teaspoon. Foreigners in the city often made contributions, but there were never sufficient funds to provide good nutrition to all who needed it. Children were seriously underfed. Alice took a sick baby to the hospital one day. The tiny girl sat for hours without moving. After a month, she was fat and healthy, active as all children should be. Alice took her back to her mother and set about finding more money for the family.

One frosty morning, Alice was talking to the cook about the food for the next day when they were interrupted by the gatekeeper. "There are some people in the courtyard who say they must see you," he told Alice. "I don't know who they are. They have never been here before."

Alice followed him to the courtyard and found a ragged, thin man and woman with a little boy shivering in the chill air. The shriveled, wrinkled skin on the woman's face gave the impression of someone very old. The man's tattered clothes hung limply on his gaunt frame.

"Please," said the man, "we have no food. Our little boy here, he will starve. Will you buy him? If he is yours, he will have something to eat. You give us money for him, and my wife and I will get something to eat until I can find work somewhere."

Alice explained that she could not accept their offer but to please step in where it was warmer. She soon returned with some bowls of rice and chunks of bread.

The woman disappeared. Alice followed her and when they went out through the gate, two smaller children sat listlessly on the ground. One squinted up through badly festered eyes. The other reached up with bony little arms covered with scabs. The mother say down beside them to hand them pieces from her chunk of bread and feed them from her bowl of rice.

"Please," she begged Alice, "they need it more than I do. They are so small, but we must sell the big boy. He eats more."

It was only the beginning of such pleas. Alice did what she could to relieve the growing distress all about the mission; but she was hampered by limitations of funds, staff, and time.

12
Arrival of the Communists

The Nationalist government's uncertain control over the country allowed increasing lawlessness across the land. More and more thieves prowled the roads and robbed homes.

The Nationalist army became increasingly desperate for more fighters, but there was no systematic program for drafting new recruits. As their soldiers marched along roads and through towns, they forcibly took any able-bodied men they could find. When a rumor spread ahead that the army was coming, the village streets immediately emptied of all but women, children, and old men. Even rickshaws stood unattended as the human power to pull them fled into hiding.

Men taken forcibly were not allowed to return home to tell their families good-bye. They simply did not come home; and, except occasionally when killed or let out of the army for some reason, their families never heard of them again.

Many of these forcibly drafted soldiers had no idea why they were fighting. No dedication to a cause inspired them, and they were often drugged to hold them in the armed forces. People were desperate.

One cold, rainy night, when Alice was staying in a house in a small village, there was a knock at the door. A ragged hungry soldier begged for food and shelter. But the family, noting that he was under the influence of drugs, was afraid that he might become violent and refused to open the door.

The next morning they found him outside the gate, frozen to death.

A bright little eight-year-old boy needed a home. His father had been taken by the army and had never been heard from again. When his mother died, he was left alone to fend for himself. He carried loads for small coppers until a rich merchant hired him for a heavy job carrying a large load into the city. Soon, the rapidly increasing inflation pushed up the cost of living, and the rich man turned him out on the street. His few coins were not enough for more than one bowl of rice.

For two days and nights, the little fellow begged on the street. He slept wherever he could find a sheltered spot. Then one of the church members told the Bible woman about him and she took him in with her. But her salary was too low to keep him and support herself. Alice was able to place him in an orphanage run by a Confucian group. He would be able to remain there for three years with a chance to go to school, and learn to spin and weave.

Naijiang swarmed with beggars. Many were small children, some blind, others with repulsive sores on hands, legs and heads. Tattered rags hung on their bony little bodies. No one dared give one of them even the smallest coin, or he would be mobbed by others. Church people discussed ways to care for these children, but the cost blocked any plan they could suggest. Alice visited one orphanage that cared for two hundred children whose fathers had been taken for the army.

An eighteen-year-old girl, helping at the church, had been married to a professional thief. When he had beaten her brutally, she had run away. Her husband threatened to kill her if he caught her. She did not dare go out on the street for fear of meeting him. Her impoverished parents had arranged her marriage before she had ever seen her husband. She had never attended school and could not recognize denominations of money.

Wartime conditions grew more threatening. One day the government closed the city gates, and they remained closed for several weeks. Supplies grew scarce. A crack in the city gate left an opening where the farmers could deliver fresh produce for the people in the beleaguered city. People at the church let baskets down over the city wall to bring up supplies.

The people at the church were realistically aware of the danger and prepared as best they could for whatever might happen. They acquired bamboo poles, and what rope they could get, to lower people over the wall behind the church property. They kept a boat tied up on the river bank beyond the wall in case they might suddenly have to take flight. They cleared out an old cistern to assure a water supply, and held fire drills. Since they might be unable to build a fire for cooking because the smoke would announce their hiding, they prepared and stored food to last for several days. Alice canned the meat of a pig.

They hid everything they valued. They packed important possessions in trunks and suitcases, and stored them in an attic over the front gate. They covered the opening with matting and hoped the looters would not notice if they came to ransack the premises. People took turns standing a four-hour watch, ready to give the alarm if looters appeared.

An order from the city came to set storm lanterns on every outside door. If a light went out for any reason after dark, someone soon arrived to reprimand and threaten punishment.

No one trusted anyone else. The person at one's elbow might be waiting for an opportunity to betray secret plans, or the whereabouts of some innocent fugitive. A knock at the door might announce someone needing a light, a Nationalist officer seeking quarters for his troops, or a ruthless looter.

The sound of Communist guns came closer and closer. More frightening was the growing suspicion and hostility toward all foreigners.

In the confusion, the women's cooperative at the Rural Industrial Center was flourishing. Fu Shi Mu, an able leader in the sewing group, was sent to the University in Chengtu for training. The Center was preparing to add spinning and dress-making to the program under her leadership.

As the Nationalist soldiers began to leave, concern grew for the young women at the Mothercraft School. No authority controlled the behavior of the departing soldiers.

One day a Nationalist troop came through Kien Yang retreating to Chengtu. They sought shelter in the schools and temples. The pastor, staying at the church to protect it, and Alice went to the Mothercraft School. When an officer demanded entrance to the school, Alice explained that there were only women there and it could not be occupied by soldiers. The officer, bayonet in hand, kicked at Alice's leg, barely missing, but hitting the door back of her until it rattled on its hinges. He screamed at her, "How can you, an American, forbid me entrance to this building?" About this time, Be Fu Sen appeared and tried to calm the officer, assuring him that what Alice said was true. They finally agreed that the men could stay in the gatehouse, but go no further.

One day, Alice stepped out into the street and found it clogged with people with clothes, bedding, and utensils piled on their backs. Those who could afford it had hired rickshaws to carry household goods. A moving mass of humanity was trying to escape to the safety of their relatives in the country.

The Communists were coming!

In some families, fathers remained behind to remove their last possessions. They preferred taking chances with possible robbers along the road to leaving anything for incoming soldiers.

Gradually the city of 10,000 became a ghost town. Doors left open to the street revealed deserted homes. Blank walls of boarded-up shops lined the empty business streets.

Rumors became increasingly ominous. People hurried through town advising, "Shut up everything and run for your life!"

But one old woman remarked, "What would they do with dry old sticks like me? We can't even build a good fire." She had no energy to walk out into the country to safety and no money to pay to be carried.

Changes came in people as well as in the government and church programs. Uncertain loyalties created feelings of insecurity.

Chou Shan Sen, a trained and experienced agriculturalist, had been baptized at the mission, and was a faithful worker on the staff. He overlooked not the smallest detail for the comfort and convenience of the two American missionaries.

When soldiers swarmed over the city, it was Wang Shih, the faithful coolie, who helped to spirit away the purebred Yorkshire pigs to safety on a farm. Chou Shan Sen had given seeds to farmers and when supplies were scarce, it was Chou Shan Sen who brought fresh vegetables from the country. Alice and Jean felt more secure knowing that Chou Shan Sen was on hand to protect them. Although they knew something was wrong, they were unable to learn what it was.

When the Nationalist soldiers left, they soaked the bridge crossing the river with kerosene. When they set it afire, volunteer firemen put it out before it reached the city. Alice was puzzled when Chou Shan Sen remarked that it wasn't important; a new concrete bridge would soon be built to replace it.

Alice's battery radio had brought the programs of the Voice of America. She had noticed that when Chou Shan Sen used the radio, he tuned it very low to programs. Suddenly she realized with a shock why so many of the people around them were becoming unfriendly, even hostile. Someone was spreading word that, as Americans, they were evil imperialists. There was a Judas in their midst. He ate with them, even attended their prayer sessions.

One day Chou Chan Sen prayed with the staff, and early the next morning, led the Communist army into the city. After that he disappeared. Posters on the church doors welcomed the Communist invaders. Chou Shan Sen had put them there to protect the church workers.

Chou Shan Sen returned one night when a staff meeting was in progress. The cook saw him and summoned Alice. When she left the meeting to talk with him, he spoke in a whisper, obviously hoping that the odor of whiskey and tobacco on his breath would not be noticed. He told Alice where he had left the money and records of his agricultural program.

He seemed depressed, tortured by conflict. He felt a genuine respect for the missionaries and their work. At the same time, he was sincerely convinced that a Communist regime would bring a golden age to his country. He believed that one could be a Christian while also being a Communist.

He was about to leave when Alice discovered that he had had nothing to eat for several days. He claimed that the liquor was to "keep up his strength." Alice's sympathy was stirred, but she was disillusioned. Here was someone who had been trusted among them. Now he turned out to be a spy, rejecting his Christian faith for political advantage. The agriculture work had played into the hands of the Communist underground to undermine the then Nationalist government.

Alice urged him to live by the Christian teachings he had accepted. He left.

For a time, Chou Shan Sen went into hiding. Then one day, he appeared again at the church to pick up his personal belongings. Later, he set up an office on the main street of town. When a church sugar cane crushing machine, purchased by the church from the Government Rural Reconstruction Commission, broke down, Chou Shan Sen stepped in to demand and obtain new rollers.

When long lines of Communist soldiers began to crowd the city and park across the river, a Communist officer appeared at the church one day. He was courtesy itself. He asked for nurses to care for their wounded soldiers stationed across the river. Their medical units, he explained, had not caught up with them. All of the local doctors and nurses had fled when the Communists had arrived. Medical supplies had been left as they fled; but later, looters had ransacked cupboards and chests, leaving behind a shambles of valuable medications and equipment strewn about the floor, broken, soiled, and unusable.

In shifts of four or five, people from the church went to the park to help with the wounded. After the impromptu nursing, the soldiers rowed the workers back across the river, gave them tea and peanuts, and astonished them with gracious expressions of appreciation.

One day, a soldier came to the makeshift medical station to demand that all of the "nurses," not then on duty, return to look after his toothache. He wanted some boric acid. He shouted and shook his fist when his demands were not immediately met. Suddenly, Chou Shan Sen appeared. Clearly he represented authority. He gave the belligerent soldier a pat on the shoulder, reassured him, and calmly led him away.

Alice never saw Chou Shan Sen again, but later heard he was in jail. His usefulness to the police was over.

The demanding soldier's attitude was later repeated when the Communist police made unreasonable claims for whatever they wanted.

The battle between the retreating Nationalists and the arriving Communists went back and forth, one side winning, then losing to the other side. The invading Communists had entered the city with great fanfare, then had beaten a hasty retreat. Welcoming signs on doors and walls disappeared to reappear again when the tide turned.

Finally, Russian-made tanks carrying United States Army equipment and filled with Chinese Communist troops rumbled along the river and crossed on the narrow ford into the city. As they roared through the streets, life went on as usual at the church, but very quietly. Special celebrations of birthdays, even Christmas plans, filled the busy calendar. But Christmas carols could not be sung openly because of the fear of arrest by police. In the church services, the robed choir sang their songs of Christian faith, their music rising in competition with the drone of planes overhead and the thud of tramping feet.

No one could guess what fate lay ahead. To their surprise, the staff at the church was not disturbed and wondered if these invaders were as unfriendly, even as vicious, toward Christianity as they had been led to believe. Perhaps the Chinese form of Communism was not the Russian type of relentless purges.

They did not know that these conquering

Communist soldiers had been carefully trained to be courteous and helpful, to enlist the support of the peasantry, and to make friends with foreigners while they were moving in to take over the country.

The Communists called it "liberation" when they took over the city. Hundreds of soldiers occupied every nook and cranny, even the church yard. They asked for supplies and utensils, but whatever they used they returned clean and in good repair. They were so different from the Nationalists, that it was difficult to believe they were from the same Chinese population. Although often poorly outfitted, they were motivated by a burning desire to fight for their cause.

The church dared not refuse them quarters; and when they were billeted in the church, they were unobtrusive and considerate. Several bedded down on the floor by Alice's bedroom door. Apprehensive at first, she soon realized that she had nothing to fear. They were respectful and polite.

Then civil rule replaced the military. Communist police, uneducated and suspicious, took over control of the city soon after Christmas. They believed in ruling by insolence and intimidation. As the soldiers left and Communist police took over, harassment and abuse began. No one could know what dangers and difficulties lay ahead.

The economy was chaotic. Silver disappeared and Communist paper money came into use. Prices soared, bouncing up and down like a yo-yo. Rice or cloth was accepted as the medium of exchange, even for bus fare. At the church, too, a stipulated amount of rice was measured out as salaries.

The effort to show that Alice and Jean, as Americans, had no advantages not enjoyed by their Chinese co-workers made no impression on the Communists. The police, often unschooled, brain-washed people from other provinces, refused to accept any concept of foreigners different from their preconceived ideas.

13
Under Communist Rule

Anyone with ideas that differed from the Communists was regarded as evil. The state, they declared, was supreme. The individual had no significance. One's worth was measured by the extent of his unquestioning obedience to authority. Lying, stealing, and killing were acceptable *if* they profited the state. One was a hero only if what they did, by hook or by crook, was of benefit to the state.

Whoever acquired wealth of whatever sort, whether by intelligence, skill, hard work, or trickery, was a capitalist. He was a parasite and killing him was justified if it advanced the interests of the state.

The Communists taught that there was no life after death, and a religious faith was disloyal to the state. The work of the church, they believed, was designed to win people to imperialistic ideas. The police told Alice and Jean that the work of the Rural Center was their job; the work of Jean and Alice was in heaven.

All American consulates in China were closed, and the personnel left the country. Word was sent to missionaries that if they stayed, they would have to look out for themselves; the United States could not be responsible for their safety. The Mission Board said that missionaries might leave if they wished; but if they remained, the Board would respect their judgment and support them morally.

Alice and Jean talked over the situation with their Chinese co-workers.

"Of course, you can leave," the co-workers replied, "but we must remain and take the abuse and dangers. You say that God called you to this work. Are you following Him or your government?"

Alice and Jean pointed out that their presence could be more of a hindrance than a help, but their co-workers said that their leaving would be a betrayal of all that the church was trying to do. There seemed to be no alternative to remaining in Kien Yang, but soon the two missionaries were placed under house arrest.

Communist restrictions limited activities everywhere. Everyone was required to wear an identifying badge to enter or leave the city. This hampered workers. Guards at the city gates were changed every day to prevent friendships which might encourage disregard of restrictions.

Unlike the Communist soldiers, the police took whatever they fancied, claiming that whatever they wanted was theirs. Officers requisitioned furniture, saying they were "borrowing" it. It was never returned and later appeared in officers' quarters. If victrolas were heard at the church, a request would soon come to "borrow" them. When asked for the radio, Alice and Jean invited the soldiers to come at any time and listen to it at the church.

But one day, an officer came to say that he only wanted the radio to listen to a special program. Hoping to avoid tension between the church and the Communist police, the church workers let him have it. Alice tried to explain how to run it, but he paid no attention to this "foreign woman," saying that he had people who knew all about it.

Some time later Alice was called. The radio was not working, and she was asked to repair it. She found that a small wire had jolted loose as it had been carried away. She made the simple connection and answered the questions about managing it, then left. She never saw her radio again.

Students and others came to the church for help. Although unable to go to the people outside their courtyard, the staff quietly held regular worship services and Bible classes. Morning prayers before breakfast, and evening prayers at bedtime, continued as usual. Christians from outside quietly came to take part.

Police arrived at the church one day to demand a room with a floor for storing rice. The only suitable place, they insisted, was the staff dining room. Alice suggested that they use an office, but they were adamant; only the dining room would do.

This room was used for meetings and as a general lounge. It was the only passageway to a busy office. Alice and Jean wisely kept out of the discussion, hoping that the Chinese staff members would be more effective in dealing with the Chinese officials. But no offer of a substitute space was accepted.

The rice was delivered to the endless monotony of the song, "Don't Be an American Slave."

The dining room tables were carried outdoors. The staff ate their meals perched on top of the sacks of rice with their heads touching the ceiling. The police guard stood by to make sure that no harm came to the rice. Typically, Alice made friends with the guard. There was rejoicing when after a month the rice was finally taken away.

During the time of storage, Alice explained that the missionaries had no other place to go. They had no permission to leave. They had always worked in their present location. She called attention to the Communist posters on the city walls promising that the government would not molest private property or churches. But the official simply shrugged his shoulders and told Alice that the rice would remain there. And since she said the church had not been able to get the return of their furniture or radio, how could they expect to have the return of any other mission property?

The official left abruptly, but soon members of the staff rushed in. "Soldiers are coming with guns!" they explained breathlessly. "They will force us to move. They say they won't even give us time to collect our clothes and personal belongings."

Alice hurried to the telephone and called the mission headquarters in Chengtu. She was told that they should remain where they were.

The soldiers never came. But it was a short reprieve. The danger of being classified as imperialists presented a constant frightening prospect.

Other property was confiscated. The church nursery at the Mothercraft School was converted into a barber shop with elaborate mirrors and chairs. Homes were confiscated and made into public thoroughfares. There was no privacy anywhere. Soldiers would suddenly appear to appropriate whatever took their fancy. Nothing was ever returned.

Taxes and forced "donations" took crops, savings, family jewelry, heirlooms, and clothes of many of the professed Christians, as well as anything else the police fancied. But the unwavering religious faith of the helpless Christian owners was a shining example of patience and forbearance.

Alice went to the police headquarters for a third time to ask for the return of her radio. With her was a seminary student who had just arrived in town and had to register at the police station. When Alice asked about her radio, the police were curt and evasive. The student tried to help, but the police demanded whom she represented. "The people," she answered.

The police pounded the desk and stamped their feet. Their faces reddened as they shouted and gesticulated. Alice and the student realized then that "the people" meant only Communists to them. Everyone else was a "foreigner" or an "imperialist." Since the student was not a Communist, they reasoned, she must be an imperialist like Alice. Both of them, they bellowed, should be shot.

Alice was ordered out of the room. The student was detained for nine hours and everyone felt deep concern for her. She was just recovering from tuberculosis. But she was allowed no rest, food, or water. When people at the church sent an egg and some hot water, she was not given an opportunity to touch them. If milk had been sent, or anything more substantial, such "luxuries" would have proved that she was an imperialist stooge.

When people from the staff tried to get into the police headquarters, they were left on the street outside. Waiting helplessly beside them were relatives of other victims who were being held inside for various "crimes" against the government.

When the student finally was released, she returned to the church to report that she had stood her ground. Her accusers had been baffled by her staunch defense of her faith. She had been compelled to sign an apology for her "attitude," but the attempt to force her to deny her Christian beliefs had failed. She realized the truth of the Bible promise that when you are called to court you need not worry about what to say, for God will give you answers. Like the situation of the early Christian martyrs, the challenge to her faith had inspired her to reaffirm it.

In West Flower Garden, the courtyard of a wealthy family was taken over by Communist soldiers. The soldiers prepared a great feast, but a band of robbers put them to flight and ate the food. When the soldiers returned later, they accused the family of being accomplices of the robbers. The young men of the household had fled, leaving only the women and an eighty-year-old grandfather. The soldiers hung the frail old man by his thumbs over a toilet pit and later threw him into jail as a hostage until the young men returned. The family and church staff members who lived on the premises had hidden, but a sixty-year-old Bible woman walked out into the courtyard with unruffled calm. She was ignored, and finally the difficulty was resolved.

Be Fu Sen's stocking knitting had not been disturbed at the Industrial Center. Then one day, an angry worker burst into a class Fu Shih Mu was teaching. "You haven't trusted me!" he declaimed hotly.

"Oh?" Fu Shih Mu answered. "Tell me what you mean, so that I can correct it."

"You Christians think you know everything," he shouted. "Our Communist leader is wiser than your Christ."

"Yes? Show him to me."

"He is Mao Tse Tung," was the defiant answer. "He is always right. He knows I should have more salary."

His unreasonable anger seemed to be a defense against an insecurity about his beliefs. Fu Shih Mu wondered if he was afraid his ideas might be wrong.

One Rural Center worker was an engineer and his wife a bookkeeper. When they began working in the church office, it became apparent that the police had access to the books. Some items brought lengthy inquiries.

Funds from the United States stopped due to the impossibility of sending money to China. Fortunately, the Chinese government needed an engineer in

Manchuria, and to the relief of all concerned, the engineer and his wife took their departure. They had a perilous trip north. They were forced to take refuge many times in a roadside ditch when fired on by enemy soldiers.

When Fu Shih Mu moved into the church quarters, the engineer and his wife had left. A Communist was on hand to claim the furniture. It belonged to the Rural Center, but it demanded Fu Shih Mu's best eloquence to persuade them to let her keep half of it.

When the police took over the Church Industrial Center, they used the large dye vats as bathtubs. They set them over the fire to heat the water, and imagination pauses modestly in contemplation of three grown men bathing together in these huge improvised "tubs"! The wooden plug at the bottom often stuck, and the used water could not be drained off to let in clean water for the next contingent of bathers.

Later, when students from school in Chengtu returned to Kien Yang, the skills they had learned in making and using dyes were put to use. But they found the dye vats in such sorry condition that time and income were lost while they were cleaned and renovated.

A new rumor reached the church. Although without their radio, the church, it was said, had set up secret broadcasting equipment to receive and send messages. On investigation, it was discovered that someone had heard the clatter of a typewriter and supposed it was the sound of a hidden broadcasting device.

The motor of the gasoline engine used to turn the washing machine gave another cause for suspicion. Someone heard the gasoline motor and notified the police. However, when the police were invited to the church to see the machine with its load of laundry for sixteen people, they were impressed. It was unbelievable that such a heavy wash could be done in such a short time without human energy. People from the street had to be invited in to feel for themselves how clean the clothes were.

Every smallest act might be cause for suspicion. One night, a student was typing a letter in English. Soldiers arrived to demand the reason for writing at night. What was she saying in another language (English), and why did it have to be written by this machine? She was questioned at length, scolded, and her letter destroyed. After that, all letters going and coming were censored.

Then Liu Yu Chen, a northern Chinese Christian, came from Chengtu to help at the church. Her calm good humor and enthusiasm lifted the spirits of everyone. She reported that the Communists in Chengtu were creating much less stress for foreigners. As spirits rose, the Chinese staff again visited homes, planned new courses of study, and set up practice nursery groups. The workers felt the warm sun of reborn courage breaking through the dark clouds that had depressed them. But Alice and Jean were still under house arrest and could not leave the church property.

Then suddenly, the police arrived to accuse Liu Yu Chen of holding meetings without permission.

"Why, I've held such meetings in the much larger city of Chengtu," she said. "There was no objection, and I've registered with the superintendent of schools there and here in Kien Yang. We have no secrets. You are welcome to visit our classes any time. There's no need to give notice beforehand."

"There must be no such other offense in the future," they admonished, disregarding the obvious fact that there had been no "such offense" at *any* time.

Liu Yu Chen knew that the difficulty had little to do with the school and its program. The problem stemmed from the growing suspicion and hostility toward foreigners. Everyone at the church became more and more apprehensive.

At the end of the school term, Liu Yu Chen applied to the county government for permission to travel to the next town to hold classes in mothercraft. Jean joined her, and they were able to get transportation in a post office truck. Because Jean was a foreigner, the truck was stopped repeatedly for inspection. Liu Yu Chen's camera was taken, and she was able to get it back only after heated arguments and signing a paper saying that she repented for having taken the camera without permission.

When they returned to Kien Yang, Jean was met by an angry policeman. She had not obtained permission to leave the city. This was the beginning of a stricter regulation: No one in any way connected with the church could leave town without police permission.

One day the town crier came down the street striking his heavy gong. Some new edict was to be announced. It soon came.

The sewers, including those behind the church property, were to be cleaned by five o'clock the next day. Anyone failing to comply would be put in jail.

Even with her frail right arm, Alice set about her share of the task. With the increasing shortage of nourishing food, and the continual demands for heavy work, her strength was ebbing. She could not manage a heavy load, but she helped to carry out the muck in baskets on poles like any other laborer. People watching observed, "There must be Communists in America, too. She is doing what they tell her to do." When she did not stop for rest with the other workers, who went inside for a nap, the police arrived and walked into the house, saying, "Get out there! How can you rest when that imperialist is out there working?"

At another time, she and Jean carried fertilizer to the country on shoulder poles. People along the street watched in amazement. Some lost their suspicions and even stopped to chat with them.

Alice and Jean were repeatedly refused permission to go to Chengtu, fifty miles away. Missionaries there and in Chungking tried to persuade the local Kien Yang police to grant the necessary permission to travel. But there was always some vague excuse to hold them under house arrest in Kien Yang. Robbers infested the roads, they were told, or the roads were too bad for travel. Sometimes they were told that "the chief of police is out of town."

The situation grew worse day by day. They had made every effort to cooperate with the new government, but to no avail. Pressures and persecution were multiplying. Should they leave, Alice and Jean wondered?

August first was declared "Anti-American Day," and the people at the church were invited to take part in a parade; but the two American missionaries were told to remain at home.

Anxious to dispel the suspicion and hostility of the new regime, the church members worked diligently on their costumes and float. The costumes won first prize for originality, but the cloud of suspicion remained as black as ever. The militant political women's society sang songs about Fu Shih Mu being a "running dog" of the Americans and called for her "liquidation."

The sixty-year-old pastor's health began to fail. He felt helpless to cope with the frightening situation if the missionaries left.

Alice and Jean well knew that their presence was

a threat to the success of the church. Yet the police blocked their departure. Was it their duty to remain at their work in the mission? Even if they could leave, would leaving be desertion in a time of crisis?

A daughter-in-law of the frail minister came to Kien Yang and stirred up feelings of insecurity and unrest, saying they *had* to work for the government. At a staff meeting one day, all but two Chinese workers present indicated a desire to leave the church and work for the government. They went to the police with written statements of their intentions. But the police laughed derisively and told them to go back home.

When his daughter-in-law left, the spirits of the ailing pastor brightened. His health improved. He began to take over his work again with renewed vigor.

Word continued to spread that the Kien Yang police were noted for their unreasonable severity. Other foreigners in China were leaving the country. Many came through Kien Yang, and Alice and Jean would have been cheered to meet and talk with someone from their own native land, speaking their own language. But such contacts would have risked suspicion that they were plotting against the government. No contacts were made.

A long succession of Communist harassments continued. Some involved minor inconveniences. Some were serious. All hindered the church work Alice and Jean were trying to carry on for the many needy people who depended on them.

Although they were made more and more to feel like *persona non grata*, any effort to leave was blocked. Their certificates from the doctor at the government's public health office were no aid in getting the necessary permit to go elsewhere. If advisable to leave, how could they manage to do so?

Bi Fu San had grown into a young teenager. He still worked at the Industrial Center. When the supply of cotton began to disappear from the storage room, the director kept watch and soon discovered that Bi Fu San was the culprit. He was working closely with the Communists. He had been so useful to them that when they had found that his wooden leg was filled with illegal silver coins, they let him go.

When he moved out of the church property, the Communists moved into his room before any other worker could occupy it. They immediately set up radio and wireless equipment, claiming that Bi Fu San had given them permission to do so. Bi Fu San and Chou San Sen were straws showing which way the wind was blowing. Life was more and more uncertain.

One day a large automobile drove up to the front gate. What now? Alice and Jean were becoming accustomed to sudden instrusions and unreasonable accusations or demands. Some of the people inside the church, working shoulder to shoulder with them, had turned traitor, reporting innocent comments or incidents to be used against them. Perhaps this was to be the final blow.

But, to their delight, it turned out to be the Chinese bishop and a fellow worker. It was a relief to pour out accounts of the indignities visited on them, but, to their dismay, the bishop held out little hope for improvement in their situation. It was all too clear that it would be best for the American workers to leave, if they could get away. The Chinese staff said that they were afraid to be left alone, yet they were reluctant to accept the fact that the presence of Americans made matters difficult, if not dangerous, for them.

If for some reason, Alice and Jean ventured out, they avoided speaking to anyone who might be placed in jeopardy because of association with these "foreign capitalists." When plans were made for a picnic for the church children, Alice and Jean were told that it would discredit the children if two foreigners were with them. It might even incur some penalty. They were prisoners of Communism and their prison was becoming smaller. It was clearly time to leave the country. But how?

Church attendance dropped. No one knew what consequences might come from identification with the church. But many remained staunchly loyal. Some blind soldiers from a military camp twenty miles away set an example of loyalty when they walked the long distance to attend services.

In times of extreme stress, everyone has a breaking point. Gentle, strong, dedicated Jean began to show symptoms of reaching that point. The heavy emotional uncertainty of the work was too much to carry. Jean needed to get away, but the police refused travel permission because the "chief is away."

Their situation was indeed critical. Finally Jean became so ill that it became urgent that she have medical help from Chengtu. At the police station, Alice broke down and sobbed uncontrollably when the request was refused. She thought Jean was dying. The astonished police gave permission for Jean to be taken to Chengtu if someone could be found to take her. Such a volunteer would certainly be in danger of arrest. Fu Shih Mu volunteered and off they went by whagger. Jean was given ten days to recover and return to Kien Yang.

A serious situation developed from a political group made up of fanatical women. The Sunday morning after Fu Shih Mu had returned from her trip to Chengtu with Jean, she was teaching her Sunday School class when she was called out by the police, and taken to the station where they accused her of claiming that there would be a third world war. She denied making any such statement. When she asked who had accused her, she learned that it had been a seamstress who lived next door to the church. She was a member of the women's organization, and her word was taken over Fu Shih Mu's. Anyone accused by another had no chance to defend himself or herself.

Fu Shih Mu was shut up in a windowless room in one of the temples occupied by the electric light company. The room was crowded with other men and women. There was no place to sit or lie down. It was the hottest season of the year, and no one was given food and only occasional sips of water. Now, they told her, she could see what hunger and poverty were like.

Every effort to gain her release met with failure. When a loyal friend tried to find evidence to prove her innocence, he was given several days of hard labor.

Fu Shih Mu was taken out and given clothes to wash. Lack of food for three days had left her so weak that she sank down in exhaustion. The church nurse was called to give her something to revive her sufficiently so that she could finish the washing.

No one from the church was allowed to communicate with her. When she needed clothing or bedding, she had to send a note by messenger, who returned from the church with the needed articles. No friendly supporter was allowed to attend her trial. When she spoke up to plead her own case, there was so much chatter and other noise in the room her voice could not be heard.

This fanatical women's society set upon the girls at the church industrial and cooperative centers with questions about the foreigners. If they refused to cooperate, they were threatened with the kind of treatment given Fu Shih Mu. Some of them were so frightened they did not risk returning to the Center for the money they had earned. Reports came that if Fu Shih Mu would tell what kind of espionage the foreigners were using, she would be set free.

There were no offenses to confess. What could be done? Alice and Jean offered to give themselves up for Fu Shih Mu if they would set her free. But, they were told, that would only make the situation worse.

Communist methods of intimidation and forced submission crippled morale and initiative. There was no defense against false accusations leveled against anyone anywhere at any time. Yet many Easter and other activities at the church were carried on as usual. Young men painted booklets with the seven last words of the Cross, and the Sunday School program and Easter egg hunt were highly successful. There was no sunrise service, as it became necessary to hold all programs at the church.

A dry year brought trouble for farmers. Fresh milk was scarce and powdered milk not available. Many crops — sweet potatoes, carrots, and cabbage — were in short supply. Although the sun shone, it did not raise the dampened spirits of the farmers, who struggled to meet the demands of the government.

As Jean's health improved, she again asked for a permit to leave China. Alice also requested permission to leave Kien Yang. But the Kien Yang police regarded both requests with indifference. Clearly the missionaries were not wanted, yet were not allowed to leave.

There seemed to be no way to break through the thick wall of suspicion and fear of everything American and Christian.

One evening, when Alice and Jean were resting on the city wall behind the church, they spoke of their dreams to float down that river to freedom. A couple of Communist soldiers joined them. Their questions held thinly veiled threats. Any answer might be

twisted to give false evidence against them.
   Was God still ruler?

14
No Way Out?

Every available space at the Rural Center was taken by Communist police and government officials. Strange men wandered in and out, even through the living quarters. They said they were "just looking around." Locked doors did not discourage them, and they might appear without warning in a bedroom. Even though a room might have space only for a bed and a chair, they claimed that it could be used for "at least twenty people."

When any of these casual intruders encountered Alice or Jean, there was no apologetic withdrawal. Rather, they burst into lusty songs praising Mao Tse Tung and exhorting all to reject slavery with America. Sometimes they sat under the windows of the church shouting endless repetitions of songs about the glories of Communism.

Notice came that the church was to be used for Communist discussion classes. Beggars, Buddhists, Christians, opium vendors, and robbers were to be eliminated from society. Guards were posted at the doors to keep the Christians out of their own property when such classes were in session. The cross and candles were removed from the altar and Communist slogans replaced them. The walls were so thin that it was not difficult to know what was going on.

The church staff thought it advisable to know what was being taught to their people. They were allowed to attend some classes and the police chief's wife, who had been successfully treated by the Rural Center's nurse, came to teach the classes. The text listed questions and answers to be memorized. Typical was, "Will there be a third world war? If not, why not?"

Answer: "No. The world is afraid of Communist armies, and the capitalist armies are so weakened by their crumbling economy that they dare not start a third world war."

Wildly distorted answers were given to many questions about America. People who disputed them were accused of disloyalty to the government. They were told that the Russians had the atomic bomb. The two missionaries were required to parrot back the answers with everyone else; to object meant more danger for their co-workers.

Brain-washing became evident everywhere. Tax collectors, farmers, government officials, farmers' wives, teachers, doctors, and nurses were required to attend lectures. The farmers had to spend so much time attending these meetings that their farms were neglected. When the police helped harvest the crops, the crops were confiscated. When the farmers asked what they would do for food, the answer was a shrug of the shoulders. Women were left little time for their spinning, weaving, and other domestic activities. Anyone not attending the lectures found it impossible to get a job.

The lectures were long and dull. They endlessly repeated, not scientific techniques for increasing production, but the merits and duties of a follower of Communism. Children were taught Communist songs and taken to sing to farmers' groups during school time. Plays and dramatic shows extolled the limitless virtues of Mao Tse Tung. They were even taught to sing, "Mao Tse Tung loves me, this I know, for his Red Book tells me so."

Families were organized into "self-criticism" groups of ten each. In their weekly sessions they were expected to confess to any "mistakes" they had made. If no confession was forthcoming, another member of the group made accusations to be answered with repentance, or punishment followed.

Even children from kindergarten age were questioned about their parents and made to confess something against them.

People were asked to purchase government bonds. The church cooperated in buying some, but the officials demanded that the church purchase more. When the pastor explained that there was no more money, he and his young assistant were taken to a meeting of merchants, who demanded that the pastor sell bonds if he did not have the money to buy them. When the pastor finally agreed that the church would purchase one hundred more, he was threatened with severe punishment if he did not produce the money immediately. The missionaries dug into their own meager reserves to meet the demand.

A Methodist hospital in a nearby city was forced to purchase one thousand bonds. One of the teachers in the Methodist school there wrote to other missionaries telling of their plight but dared not speak openly of the difficulties. He wrote this parable, the meaning a challenge to the good Bible student:

There were two ladies of the Wesleyan persuasion living in a far country. They sent a friend to the institution mentioned in Luke 19:25 to ask whether or not the operation on Job 28:17 could be performed upon their grass-colored backs. The answer was what one's speech should be according to the first part of Matthew 5:37. Well satisfied, the next day, they sent as many as the man in the parable had sheep and received not the root of all evil, but only the first of two things 2 John 12 would not write with, named after the bustable things of Jeremiah 5:5. They had designated for this purpose, twice as much as Malachi commanded to be brought into the storehouse, thinking this would bring to them what, according to the King James translation, the angels announced for all men in Luke 2:14. But the institution demanded for these perishable things as much as Abraham gave to Isaac (Genesis 25:5). The same evening, the institution of Luke's profession received something similar to Esther 1:19 to the effect that said institution must possess itself of as many of these things as were chased by one in Joshua 23:10. Since the state of the institution was as that of the debtors in Luke 7:42, having already possessed itself of sixty-seven, the request of 1 Kings 12:13 was made, but the man they were dealing with proved to be a Shylock.

One day a Christian from the West Flower Garden arrived in breathless distress. "Yang Chiou Shih," he reported, "is in jail. She is accused of robbery."

Yang Chiou Shih was a teacher in the Rural Center nursery school. She had received a letter, supposedly from a family who had been driven from their home where the nursery school had been held. The police had closed and sealed the house. The teacher had never seen this letter, which the police had intercepted. Yang Chiou Shih was given a permit to return for school equipment left there. However, when she returned, they demanded that she produce clothing and papers they knew were not there. It would appear to be robbery.

The penalty for robbery was death. People at the church signed a bond for her release, and after grueling questions she was set free. Whatever gain had been expected for the Communists was lost in sympathy for the victim of this trickery. Yang Chiou Shih had not considered herself a Christian, but she began to see the advantages of Christianity over an ideology that would resort to the kind of indignities she had suffered.

Many people attending services and working on the church programs did not call themselves Christian. But they valued what they observed as they worked with the Chinese Christians and missionaries who set an example of applied Christianity in tolerance, fair play, and compassion.

One morning, the police arrived while the church staff was having breakfast. They took the minister to another room.

"We have proof that you have silver," they accused him. "You must tell us where you got it and when. Also, how much do you have in your possession now?"

"Why, I don't have any silver," answered the minister in surprise.

The officers sat down, saying they would wait until he "confessed." Other members of the church staff came into the room.

"How can we help?" one of them asked. "We know that our minister has broken no rules."

But the minister represented the church and was the target of interest. Finally, the officers rose to go. "We're leaving now," they said, "but we'll be back tomorrow. You had better be ready to make a confession then, or we'll take you to jail."

The pastor was sixty years old and in frail health. It

was doubtful that he could survive the hardships in jail.

That night the staff met to pray and consider their position. Quite likely, someone had attended the Sunday morning worship service and dropped some silver coins into the offering plate. This would provide evidence that the minister had silver, and only he could be held to account. All present at the staff meeting signed a statement declaring that they had no silver and would not use it in the future.

The next morning the tension mounted. But the police did not come.

This was typical of Communism: Keep people so anxious they would be ready to submit to orders. Nothing was ever settled. Crippling anxiety kept everyone feeling that a Sword of Damocles hung overhead ready to fall at some unexpected moment.

There seemed to be no way to avoid stress with the local police. Unreasonable demands and trumped-up charges increased. The police harassed the church nurse with endless irrelevant questioning. They hampered her work at the West Flower Garden. The worker's religion was ridiculed; but her staunch, unwavering faith in her Christian beliefs baffled and enraged her questioners.

One day, Alice sat at the bedside of Lee Shan Sen, the seminary student who had been questioned by the police in the radio incident. They talked about the message she was to give in church the following Sunday.

Other staff members across the courtyard saw an eavesdropper crouched under the window. The soldier, ignorant and supersitious, did not understand anything that was said. He rushed into the room and demanded that Lee Shan Sen get up and go to the police station. With his gun leveled at her, Lee Shan Sen calmly powdered her nose and combed her hair. Alice tried to follow them when they left, but was roughly shoved back. An hour later Lee Shan Sen returned, smiling broadly. The police had "made a mistake," she reported, and she had been set free.

Neighbors reported that the police were especially angry with the church staff because they were "living in luxury." Intentionally reduced to bare necessities by American standards, they had tried to conserve energy and live frugally, but wisely. They knew they would probably need every ounce of physical stamina to hold steady in the heavy stress in which they lived. With careful budgeting and wise economies, it was possible to live simply, but follow a sensible routine. Many people were deliberately letting their clothes become ragged, even dirty, to prove that they were living without luxuries.

A local business woman made every effort to prove that she was not an undesirable capitalist. She went to the fields as a common laborer two or three days a week. Members of her family cleaned the jail, emptying toilet buckets and scrubbing floors.

But the Communists arrested her aging father on false charges of gun possession. At the jail he asked what a gun was; he had never seen one. But even if he didn't know anything about a gun, he did know something about his book, he said. It was his Bible. When the police insisted that he had guns hidden somewhere, he bowed with his hands tucked into his sleeves.

"Well," he replied calmly, "I guess I'll just have to sit here and wait for the honorable gentlemen to decide what to do with me, because I don't have any guns." He opened his Bible and began to read. The name on the flyleaf was the same as the name of one of the two soldiers. The attitude suddenly changed. They were unable to intimidate the old man and finally dismissed him. He bowed graciously, thanked them for their kindness to such an unworthy old man, and took his departure.

Tensions tightened. Rumors continued to grow and multiply. Although many of them were absurd, they undermined confidence. Anxious people withdrew from church classes. At the Industrial Center, those who remained were proud of their embroidery, children's clothes, and the toys they made, but more than half of them slipped away with some lame explanation for leaving. With the diminishing receipts from abroad, the pupils remaining could not provide sufficent funds to keep the work going.

There seemed to be no way out.

15
Permission to Leave

At last, Alice and Jean were called to talk with the wife of the chief of police. She asked them when they wanted to leave. They answered, "as soon as possible," and were astonished when she suggested the following day. They had been packed and ready to leave at a moment's notice, but had been waiting for the police permit and transportation. Now, apparently, permission was to be granted.

They had made a carefully itemized list of everything they had from a pin to a camera. When the police came to inspect their baggage, they thumbed through each of their books, page by page. They insisted that Alice and Jean remove their shoes to show anything illegal that they might have packed in with their feet. Co-workers stood by to help repack when the inspection was finished. Alice was happily surprised when her camera was not confiscated.

The best available transportation was a small boat, rowed some of the time, poled some of the time. The price was unreasonably high, but the luggage was loaded aboard; and after prayer with the mission staff, Alice and Jean started down the street on their way to the waterfront. Their spirits were high. It was to be the first lap of their long journey to freedom.

Suddenly their progress was halted by a policeman who came running after them. "You cannot leave today," he said. "You must wait two more weeks." He gave no explanation.

There was nothing to do but return to the church. When they sat down to eat their lunch, a policeman was standing by.

The baggage had to be left on the boat. Most of the passage payment had been made, but the boatman said that he had had to buy provisions for the journey so he could not return any of it.

The police said that they would have to get travel permits from a "higher authority." Fourteen missionaries were being held at the next stop on their journey, the police said; but Alice knew that there had been only five, and they had already left.

The wife of the chief of police again came to their rescue. She advised the two stranded missionaries to write out their purpose for leaving and appear the next day. When the statement was presented, they were told that it must be written in more scholarly language.

That night the pastor of the church rewrote it, and Alice appeared at the police station early the next morning. It was raining and chilly, but the day seemed bright to Alice. She received the coveted permit, even though it was only to go as far as the next "authority" station.

On August 25, 1950, Alice and Jean, followed by fifty Christians, set out for the boat. The rain poured down as they made their way to the little boat. It was crowded to capacity. Alice and Jean sat and slept on their baggage piled on the deck in the center of the boat. The wife of the boatman cooked at one end over a tiny charcoal burner. The toilet was the side of the boat. Bath and drinking water came from the same river. A scanty awning over the center of the boat served for protection from the sun and rain.

Faithful Chang Shih, from the church, had come

with them to help when needed. Sometimes he rowed or poled. Alice and Jean tried to crouch down where they would not be seen and stopped for questioning or more baggage inspection.

A week later, they arrived in Neichang. They went to the police station to ask for a travel permit to take them to the next point on their journey. With excuses and evasions, the permit was not forthcoming and they had to wait two weeks before leaving. Other travelers had gone through without delay. No one could explain why Alice and Jean were scolded unreasonably for their enforced stay. They were called liars and, without explanation, told to wait. Seemingly, orders had come from someone to make things as difficult as possible, probably because they were foreigners.

Two days after leaving Neichang, their little craft met the waters of the great Yangtse River at Chungking. They went immediately to the office of the police. The next morning, officers came to the boat to ask questions and examine their baggage.

The police told them that they must leave their boat and stay in a "modern hotel." It had a mud floor with rat holes along the walls and under the bed. The proprietor was a Christian and made every effort to assure their comfort. He sold them their tickets for their steamboat trip to Hangkow. At the police station, their questions about time of stay and other details met with indifferent, curt answers.

Chang Shih helped to buy food from street vendors. But soon it was advisable for him to return home to Kien Yang. It pulled painfully on heart strings to bid him good-bye. It meant severing warm, close ties with work and people dear to them. They heard later that Chang Shih had arrived safely. They longed for word, too, of Fu Shih Mu. They knew that the Political Women's Society was determined to destroy her; but they never heard of her again, even in the years to come.

Alice had been suffering with a throbbing toothache. During the last delay before reaching Chungking she was able to locate a dentist and have it extracted. The local newspaper printed an item about their presence in town, and requested that if anyone knew of a reason why they should not be allowed to leave the country, it should be reported. No one appeared with accusations, so they prepared once again to continue their journey. After another thorough baggage inspection, they boarded a little steamer and took their places with their luggage on deck.

The weather was beautiful and their spirits rose. Sixteen other missionaries had just left. It appeared that Alice and Jean had been detained to prevent any contact with other Americans who might carry back to the United States discrediting reports of the new regime in China. Arriving in Chungking, they were met by missionaries, but delayed another two weeks. They were allowed to stay with the Stockwells.

Then, as they floated down the Yangtse River, they were put up in a cabin where they could look out over a breathtaking panorama of gorges and cloud-capped peaks. The reflection of mountains wavered in the sun-flecked foam that stirred on the glassy surface of the river. Rocky walls towered on either side, dwarfing the small figures of boatmen in their river craft below. Those same mountains had looked down on men going up and down the great river before the days when Confucius uttered his philosophical words of morality and religion.

They were thankful for the skilled pilot. He never took his eyes from the river as the boat was carried on with the relentless speed of the current. He had lived and worked all his life along the river and knew its every mood.

From spectacular gorges they came out on a land suddenly flat and treeless. For a day and a night, they sailed past flat land so flooded that there seemed to be no banks between the river and the fields. No houses were to be seen for vast expanses of motionless water. It was the annual flood.

They were exhausted when they finally reached Hangkow. At the next stop, a Canadian missionary met the boat. He provided invaluable help in working with the police for the permits to continue on their journey. Then their hopes were dashed anew. Their permits had run out, they were told, because of their delay in Chungking.

Detailed questions consumed long hours. They stayed with British missionaries at the China Inland Mission. Their hosts were required to vouch for their good behavior while in the city. They, too, were awaiting exit permits, but would not be allowed to leave until the Americans had gone.

It was difficult to get word from or to the United States. Money had to be obtained at the post office or British Consulate. The American consul had left months before.

Their hosts kindly paid bail for Alice and Jean so they might go about freely until permitted to continue on their way. They enjoyed a lovely room with delicious food, and were immeasurably grateful not to have to put up in a hotel as they had had to do in Neichang for two weeks. It seemed eons of time since they had left Kien Yang and it continued to rain dismally.

While waiting in the lovely China Inland Mission home, Alice and Jean saw a new part of China. It was difficult to believe that only a day's journey upriver everything was so different. Here they could buy anything from Lux soap to American food of all kinds.

Alice and Jean enjoyed the luxury of shampoos. As for other American women, it was a morale booster. They also enjoyed a well-produced play about Communist China.

Days stretched into weeks. The suspense was exhausting. An officer would wander into the house at any time, unannounced, demanding a detailed report of all that the travelers had said or done the previous day.

Missionaries from other parts of China were arriving, hoping, like Alice and Jean, to leave the country. After a month's delay, they were finally told to be ready to leave the following morning by train. It had been two and a half months since they had left Kien Yang. They had had eight baggage inspections and were fortunate to have lost only a few "forbidden articles."

They finally boarded the train that took them south from Hangkow to Canton. They left Canton in the morning and reached the border between China and the British New Territory in the afternoon. A bridge marked the boundary.

They found the baggage they had checked in Hangkow. One set of coolies carried it to the inspection point, another to the bridge center, another to the Hong Kong side, and another to the train for Hong Kong. There was only a hurried examination.

The attitude of the people on the Hong Kong side of the bridge was startling. It seemed like going from a black hole out into bright sunshine. It was difficult to adjust from suspicion to warm friendliness. A policeman smiled voluntarily and asked a friendly question. It seemed strange not to fear being misunderstood.

They hurried to the train for Hong Kong and rode in state in the observation car. They had telegraphed ahead, but their train was six hours late. Alice's Szechwan Chinese was not understood in southern China, but the cheerful young man who met them at two o'clock in the morning spoke English.

For the first time after what seemed like a lifetime, Alice and Jean walked on free soil. The air was free; speech was free; thoughts were free; actions were free. No police came and went everywhere at all hours with endless questions. There were no trumped-up charges of crimes never committed, no arrests of innocent people on the word of some malicious informer, no jails crowded with human beings robbed of privacy, human necessities and their liberty.

Alice and Jean had longed to leave Communist China, but now that they were doing so, they discovered that they were leaving something of themselves behind in the vast changing land where they had given their best efforts to show the Christian way of life. They knew the potential of a great people struggling through staggering problems.

The very air seemed different on the other side of the bridge marking the border between Communism and freedom. The tensions under Communism had seemed to create an acrid odor.

Still feeling uncertain, wondering what might happen next, Alice began to breathe clean, fresh air. No one was going to question her, threaten her, or falsely accuse her of some unknown crime.

Freedom! How sweet it was!

They found that they could sail from Hong Kong on a British freighter. It would take forty days to reach Liverpool, but it would cost less than crossing the Pacific because of favorable exchange on the English pound. They would go by Genoa, Italy, and from Italy to England, then on to New York. They would miss a cherished dream of Christmas with loved ones at home.

The last lap of the trip from London to New York on the Dutch liner, *S.S. Veendam*, seemed endless. Most of the six hundred Europeans of various nationalities on board ship were emigrating to the United States. Few spoke English or only spoke it brokenly.

Jean and Alice were exhausted and homesick. It had been five months since leaving Kien Yang, five months of strain, uncertainty and danger, five months of tension and unexplained delays and false accusations.

Both Alice and Jean were ill. They had gone to China with a high purpose. Had their mission failed? Tired, weak and ill, did they feel defeated in their hopes of carrying Christian good will to a country just emerging into world importance? Was the sacrifice of hundreds of lives and the dedication of hundreds of missionaries to the work of the gospel in China in vain? Many would be tempted to say "yes." But those who had seen the work of the Holy Spirit in Chinese lives knew full well that what God had begun in them would be carried on. With China closed to the outside world, they would wait and see. (Philippians 1:6)

Alice and Jean's lives were not closed books.

16
A Different Land, A Different Opportunity

When Alice arrived back in the United States, the long months of strain, poor food and physical deprivations had taken their toll.

Medical tests showed serious loss of weight. Five intestinal parasites drained her strength, and she suffered severe nervous tension. At first unable to sleep, she finally slept for days. Gallbladder surgery drained away more strength but brought better health.

Jean's health improved and eventually she went to teach in Japan. Later, she married happily and lived in California.

After a year and a half Alice continued to feel the urge to go to a foreign country with the message of her Christian faith. Her interest was drawn to the Philippines. Then she attended a Christian Education Conference in Nashville, Tennessee, where she met a missionary on furlough from the Central American Republic of Costa Rica. The account of a planned rural center there stirred her enthusiasm. She had continued her contacts with the Mission Board in New York, and she wrote them of her interest in a post somewhat like the one she had known in China.

The more she found out about Costa Rica, the more it seemed to beckon her. She learned that it was a peaceful little country between Nicaragua and Panama in the chain of Central American republics. Costa Ricans were proud of spending more on education than on the army, with more school teachers than soldiers. A popularly elected president with no body guard or secret service escort walked the streets of the capital city of San Jose like any private citizen.

People along the Pacific and Atlantic coasts were mostly blacks and Indians while the population of the inland plateau was largely of European descent with fair complexions and dark hair and eyes.

In 1917, George A. Miller, superintendent of the Panama Mission, had made a trip to Costa Rica, accompanied by a Mexican minister, Eduardo Zapata. Together they explored the country where there had never been any Methodist work before. They purchased a clubhouse in downtown San Jose, remodeled it for a church and called it "El Redentor" (Church of the Redeemer). Its offices became Methodist headquarters. Soon an excellent school was under way, later relocated in the newer section of the growing city.

The work had grown steadily. Alice learned that there were eighty-three preaching places scattered over the country. Her experience and skills in religious education, program organization, and evangelism were needed everywhere.

Communism had met a solid wall of opposition when attempting to infiltrate the peaceful little country with its mild climate and democratic way of life. What a change from vast China with its turmoil of clashing forces and upheaval of change! But she was soon to recognize that every opportunity brings its problems.

Two years to the day from November 1, 1950, when she had arrived in Hong Kong, leaving the country of her life's dedication, she landed on November 1, 1952, on the Caribbean coast of Costa Rica in the steaming little port of Puerto Limon. As she stepped ashore from the United Fruit Company boat that had brought her from New York, she felt the oppressive, sticky heat of the tropics. She would not feel the chill of winter again for a long, long time to come.

Lines of swarthy black men moved from low, open freight cars on the dock to the side of the ship where they rolled huge bunches of green bananas from their shoulders onto the canvas conveyor belt taking the States-bound fruit over and down into the ship's hold. Alice learned that the United Fruit Company owned the largest fleet of refrigerated boats in the world.

An American missionary met her and reported that good fortune smiled on them. "The trains to San Jose just began running again today," he said. "Floods had washed out the tracks." He mopped his brow and guided her to the small railroad station.

The train trip and her missionary escort provided further acquaintance with Costa Rica. Nine months of the year it rained. A gentle breeze cooled the air during the "dry season." Bougainvillea covered pastel-painted farmhouses. Flowers blossomed everywhere, showers of orchids dripped from spreading trees. Monkeys, iguanas, alligators, anteaters, and brightly plumed birds enjoyed the thick jungle growth, sometimes crowding on either side of the railroad tracks.

Oxcarts with gaily painted solid wooden wheels lumbered along the country roads, bringing farm produce to town markets. Coffee, sugar cane, cacao, pineapples, and bananas flourished in the rich soil and generous rainfall. Fence posts along the country roads were "planted" so they would take root and sprout. This avoided their rotting in the rich, damp soil.

Alice took up residence at the language school in San Jose, where she remained for nine months. She had three months more to complete the usual year of study when the missionary in the town of Palmar Sur asked for her help with work he was opening in the little town of Golfito on the Pacific coast.

She left the language school to meet the urgent need. Vast banana plantations covered the countryside, and Alice was quartered on the second floor of one of the laborer's shacks. On the first floor, drunken workers came and went, carousing and fighting most of the night.

One day she opened the door to find one of the most beautiful Costa Rican girls she had ever seen on the doorstep. Lovely black hair framed her fair features. Large black eyes looked out in tearful entreaty.

"Please, I don't know what to do!" she burst out as Alice led her indoors. "My name is Ester Gamboa. I don't want to go on any longer. My husband and I are divorced. The only work I have been able to get is housework, but people say dreadful things about me because I have no husband. What can I do?" she sobbed.

She was to join the long line of unhappy, troubled, and lonely people Alice mothered over the years.

When Alice returned to continue her language study in San Jose, she made steady progress. While in Golfito she had used her tape recorder to lead the music in her services and practiced preaching into it, listening for mistakes as she replayed it. Children who came to the meetings were candid critics, and she learned a great deal from their good-natured corrections.

After completing her language study, she took up her work in the town of Ciudad Quesada, located only a short distance from the Nicaraguan border. The

American pastor of the church made no effort to conceal his disappointment in having a woman instead of a man as a co-worker. Although Alice had full ordination as a minister, women were not yet accepted cordially in the clergy profession.

Townspeople's hostility toward Protestantism registered in curses from adults and rock-throwing from children. When the American pastor took a seriously ill woman to the hospital in his automobile, he was reviled for "riding over the body of Christ" because he had driven an automobile on Good Friday. Later, a bomb was set off in his car. Luckily, no one was in it at the time. But the much-needed car was completely demolished.

The mission acquired a considerable acreage of land five miles from town. It was to be developed into the San Carlos Rural Center. It became a demonstration farm for crop improvement, conducting research to find the best cattle feed for nearby farmers. Purebred cattle from the States were brought to upgrade local stock. Buildings were erected for summer youth camps, institutes, workshops, retreats, and study centers. The income from the farm would help toward self-support.

Energetic, plucky little Virginia Lane joined Alice. Together they planned their own house at the Rural Center. Local carpenters were amazed at the strange ideas of a combined bathtub and shower and two rooms joined by a wall with built-in cupboards. A local carpenter put up a wall cupboard which immediately fell down. He blamed Alice because she had "put things in it." When he took off, leaving the job unfinished, Alice and Virginia took up hammer and saw and completed the job.

Costa Rican neighbors were quick to copy attractive ideas. They purchased better roosters and raised better chickens from the high-grade eggs available at the farm.

Alice was delighted to find a fresh peach from the United States in the market. It cost thirty-seven cents for the one peach, but had little resemblance to the small, green, hard ones from local farms. The long rainy season allowed no rest period for the trees.

She showed farm women how to can fruits and vegetables, working with them to put up tomatoes, pineapples, mangoes, and other produce.

Later, missionaries supervised the building of a dam to create a pond for breeding fish. It was a long and tedious task, but the deep water for the tilapia fish, an Asiatic pan fish, provided a new source of protein as well as an additional source of income for the Rural Center. Almost immediately, neighbors began to copy the dam to make ponds on their own property for cultivating a fish crop.

Work in the church in Ciudad Quesada grew unevenly. A strong women's society supported several projects, and the Sunday School grew. Church attendance fluctuated. Sometimes a good congregation gave hope for a bright future. Then for some reason, attendance dropped.

The American pastor built walls and a roof around and over the local house where meetings were held. When completed, he removed the house inside and had a completed church.

There was no one to play the piano for worship services, but a worker with the Seventh Day Adventists helped to train a choir that could sing without accompaniment. Later, the wife of a missionary at the farm taught piano lessons to a few eager pupils.

The priest who had planned the bombing of the pastor's car later presented him and Alice with Certificates of Honor for organizing 4-H Clubs throughout the area. The boy who actually placed the bomb in the car later joined the church.

Alice and Virginia Lane alternated weeks, one remaining to help on the farm and in the Ciudad Quesada Church; the other to make the trip into the interior for services in outlying towns and villages.

On those trips, Alice rode horseback much of the time and slept in her sleeping bag on the floor of palm-thatched huts when invited to stay. She traveled steep mountain trails, dangerously slippery from torrential rains. Trucks along the back country roads were often held up by landslides.

Swollen rivers often overflowed their banks. She crossed innumerable rushing streams where there were no bridges and the water came up above the stirrups. Snakes sometimes fell from trees overhead and often slithered over the ground underfoot. Life held dangers, but different dangers from those she had known at her former mission post.

"Time goes and goes and goes and I go and go and go, but somehow time always wins the race," Alice wrote her Aunt Tee. "Anyway, I have been to Glory (a small town) and back, and am getting ready to go on to the river. We have a new motor for a boat, so we should have a lot of fun. It took two to three days to row upstream before.

"Last week I took Star (her mare) and her colt. The rainy season is beginning but the mud isn't deep, just slick. Star fell twice. The first time I had time to get off and let her up. She had never fallen for me before. The second time I jumped off quickly, but she couldn't get up even with me off and ended with her head downhill and three feet waving in the air with the saddlebags under her where we couldn't get them off. A man came to my rescue. He yanked up on her tail until she got her back feet under her; then up she came. I thought for a while she was a dead horse for she just lay there groaning and wouldn't move. The colt was a brave little fellow, and I think I'll call him Valiente, meaning valiant.

"I walked the rest of the way to Glory and only had Star carry the bags. When we had to cross a river, I sent Star across alone and hiked across on a log further down. She crossed the swift part safely but when little Valiente entered the water, the current picked him up and carried him like a chip of wood. He was mighty surprised but caught his feet on a rock and waded directly upsteam and was soon on firm ground. I'm going to give Star a good feed of corn. How she likes bananas! She will do anything for them.

"On my return, as I was nearing the farm, I heard a big explosion. When I arrived, I found that lightning had struck one of the big trees between our houses. It made a hole at the root of the tree and burned out the fuse for the lights in the house, melting a rim on the bulb in the bathroom. Needless to say, everybody had a shock. I wish we'd get lightening rods, but they're expensive and the head of the farm thinks the aluminum roof will protect us.

"I'm thankful for the screens at the Center. I can sit here and write without seeing a single bug . . ."

Alice was able to get a jeep with a canvas top. When she went for her driver's license in San Jose, she had difficulty understanding the examiner's questions. She laughed at her blunders and tried successfully later.

Twenty purebred little heifers arrived from a generous California cattleman. Not one was more than six months old. Since there was no known remedy for the tropical tic fever, only young cattle growing up with their own immunity could survive when brought from a temperate climate.

The airplane bringing the heifers was an old prop jet which had been gutted to make room for stalls. With no air conditioning and flying 20,000 feet above tropical storms, the little calves arrived weak and sniffling with colds. Trucks met the plane at the San Jose airport and soon had them at the San Carlos Center, under the care of the missionary expert in animal husbandry. As they grew to maturity they would be bred to native cattle and upgrade the livestock throughout the district.

One day when driving the eighty miles to San Jose, Alice and some co-workers had gone only halfway when they were stopped by a policeman. He asked them what was happening in Ciudad Quesada.

"Why, nothing unusual," Alice answered. "Everything was all right when we left a short time ago."

But much had happened.

No wall, fence or other visible barrier marked the border between Nicaragua and Costa Rica. Some Nicaraguan soldiers had casually walked down the road into Ciudad Quesada, handcuffed the half dozen local police and cut the communication lines to San Jose.

As Alice and her passengers drove on, they met the entire Costa Rican army going to the rescue of Ciudad Quesada. It was made up of one truckload of police from San Jose and the little town of Alajuela.

The "war" in Ciudad Quesada lasted three days. Shots were fired, not at each other, but at lamp posts in the central plaza and the walls of buildings, making sure that no one was hit. One elderly man was accidentally shot while crossing the street.

When the Nicaraguan soldiers tried to move on into Costa Rica from Ciudad Quesada, they were refused food and shelter everywhere by indignant farmers. They had to retreat back into their own country.

17
Costa Rica

As Alice became fluent in Spanish, her third language, she was often asked to take over the work of one of the missionaries leaving on furlough. She had been in Cuidad Quesada three years when she was sent to the lovely little town of Alejuela, twelve miles from San Jose. The attractive little Methodist church was located strategically on the main plaza of town.

The house built as a parsonage a few blocks from the church, and occupied by the missionary on furlough found her alone, a stranger, on Christmas Eve. She had not yet become acquainted. The Christmas church programs had been held on December 23. The noisy plaza celebrations of December 24 and 25 would have disrupted any activity at the church. She had always had warm ties to those around her and felt desolate to spend Christmas alone. Kind neighbors brought holiday food, but she longed for the closer warmth of the human fellowship on which so much of her life was built.

At first, the congregation was uneasy with a woman pastor. But as time went on, her warm personality brought enthusiastic acceptance of her leadership.

One of her new acquaintances was to be a lifelong

friend and became another in the long line of people Alice mothered.

Helen Hoyt was an American school teacher from California. She had gone to Alajuela on retirement and had bought a delightful little Spanish-style house. Kitchen, living room, and bedrooms all opened around an orchid-filled patio. Alice was to make her headquarters with Helen for the rest of her years in Costa Rica.

Someone gave Alice a tiny puppy. Alice named her Lucy. She could stand with all four little feet on the palm of Alice's open hand. She never grew larger than an average cat and traveled with Alice on her horseback trips into the interior, her little head peering over the edge of the market basket which she considered her personal property. She sat quietly under Alice's chair during meetings.

When Alice told Helen Hoyt about Lucy, Helen said that under no circumstances would she have a dog in her house. Alice suggested that Lucy, with her good manners, be allowed to be a guest only for three days. Helen reluctantly agreed. On the second day, Alice returned from a meeting to find Lucy curled up on Helen's lap, firmly established as an accepted member of the household.

Alice was appointed Conference Director of Christian Education. She visited the numerous outlying communities where new churches needed assistance in organization. She conducted vacation Bible schools and trained numbers of young people for lay leadership.

George A. Miller had been elected to the Episcopacy by the General Conference of 1924 and assigned to Methodist work in Spanish America. He had worked tirelessly to promote self-support and national leadership, leaving each of his Episcopal areas — Mexico, Argentina, and Chile — under the supervision and control of "nationals." The growing need for trained ministers as well as lay workers was urgent. The seminary in Argentina met many of those needs in the southern part of the Spanish American field, but a similar training school was needed for workers to the north.

In 1957, after retirement, Bishop Miller went to Costa Rica to study the possibilities of building such a school there. A committee of missionaries and church leaders joined him in the selection of the best location. Property was chosen on the outskirts of quiet little Alajuela, twelve miles from the crowds and distractions of San Jose.

Bishop Miller purchased the land with his own savings, and returned to California to raise the funds for the first building to be used for a dormitory and classrooms. Later he worked with Samuel Guy Inwood, a famous church architect, on plans for a chapel which he gave to the school in memory of his beloved wife, Margaret Ross Miller.

The school was named "Escuela de Preparación para Obreros Metodistas" (Methodist School for Training Christian Workers) — EPOM. Young people came from various parts of Costa Rica and Panama to train for work in their local churches.

It was a crucial time of need for the kind of work Alice's training and experience had equipped her to do. She taught classes in religious education, Bible study, and rural church work. She was also a valuable counselor for the young men and women coming to the school.

In 1959 Bishop Miller, at the age of 91, again made the trip to Costa Rica for the dedication of the new chapel. Helen and Alice had put on the finishing touches with skillful campus landscaping. They used native shrubs and flowers.

It was a great day for Costa Rican Methodists when

the chapel was dedicated. Methodists gathered from far and wide for an all-day celebration. Alice wrote her aunt: "We have had the dedication program for the new chapel at the Training School. Churches from all around San Jose and Alajuela came with all their Sunday Schools and held their classes on the lawn under the trees. Then there was a picnic lunch and a time of singing and testimony. This was followed by the dedication service in the chapel. Only some of the adults could enter, for there were about five hundred people here. The children and the rest of the adults sat on the terraces and listened to the service over the loudspeaker. It had been raining every day about 12:00 noon, so we were more than pleased when the rain held off until about 3:00 p.m., when everyone had left for home.

"How wonderful things work out with the Lord's blessing! Monday night there was the dedication of another new church building at Guadalupe near San Jose. The church there, too, was overflowing into the street."

A new church in Alajuelito ("little Alajuela") followed; then others, as the Costa Rican work grew.

Trained leaders and laymen were of immense importance to the Costa Rican church. All but three of four of the pastors for the churches for the next twenty years were to come from this school.

One of them was Ester Gamboa, who came to serve Alice and Helen as a housekeeper to earn the support of her two children while she studied at EPOM. She became pastor of the little church of Pueblo Nuevo near Golfito. After graduation and several years of service in the churches in Costa Rica, she moved to New Jersey in the United States. She married happily and continued to be active in the Spanish-speaking churches there. One daughter became a trained nurse in California and married there. The other daughter married a Costa Rican minister who became president (the equivalent of a bishop in the United States) of the Costa Rican Methodist Church.

A man in a remote interior locale bought a Bible from a traveling colporter. He was the only person in his community who could read, and was astonished at what he read. Leaving his isolated place in the jungle, he traveled down the alligator-infested river to seek help from a missionary in Golfito. A group of Golfito young people returned with him. Along the way, hot and tired, they decided to take a swim. Their leader took off in the water but never returned. No one ever discovered what had happened.

The group continued on their way, sobered and saddened. People from the surrounding country echoed their feelings and came to the services where many reponded to the message the young people brought. Later, several of the liquor and gambling establishments closed, and a church began to grow. One young man attended the training school in Alajuela, graduated, and later became a church district superintendent with headquarters in San Jose.

On Alice's return from a furlough in the States, she drove a jeep station wagon all the way from Detroit to Costa Rica. Two cousins followed in another car. The Panama Highway had only been completed for occasional short distances. Many roads were little more than rough, unpaved paths. Some streams had no bridges. They encountered only one border difficulty. A drunken guard at the Guatemala point of entrance insisted that they "surely wanted to" turn around and go back to the States. Appeals to the local police finally brought permission to proceed.

The jeep was invaluable when Alice reached Costa Rica and journeyed out over the country in her work with Sunday Schools, women's groups, and growing church congregations.

Alice set up and managed the sorely needed bookstore on the Training School campus. When she needed additional supplies not available in Costa Rica, she decided to drive her jeep station wagon to Panama, taking Ester and her two children with her. The only "road" was the River Sierpe, winding its crooked way through the impenetrable, matted jungle between Costa Rican farmlands and the border of Panama. What road there was had fifty-two river crossings. Alice and her passengers sometimes rode with water up to their knees inside the jeep.

They passed other cars in serious difficulty. In one place people stood hip deep in a line across a stream to guide vehicles through shallow places and around hidden rocks. Where large cars had trouble, the humble jeep could get through.

One night, when there was nowhere to sleep, Alice bedded down on top of the jeep with her passengers doubled up inside as best they could manage. The next morning, they tied up to a car stuck in the stream and hauled it to the bank.

In a later letter Alice wrote, "The dry season is over and the rains have really arrived. The garden in the patio is like a lake. The street is like a river because the water can't run off fast enough.

"This morning I went to a place where I had not been before. Two students went with me. There is no church there, but a few people wanted to hear more about the gospel. We followed the road to Poas, the volcano, to a little town where we went directly to a home where they received us cordially. We talked a while and the lady of the house bought a Bible. The man of the house wasn't there but came in later and shouted for us to get out or he'd shoot us full of holes. He grabbed his revolver, loaded it, and waved it at us. His wife and daughter apologized in tears as we took a quiet departure." Later the family attended the church.

In another letter, Alice described a typical trip to a small town. "We have had a pastors institute here in a little country church," she wrote. "The people themselves built a parsonage onto the little church where there is now a school of about forty children. The government is supplying the teacher until a public school can be built. Twelve pastors attended the institute, plus eighteen lay leaders. It lasted for three days. I stayed on to visit several other churches and meet with Sunday School teachers. I spent two days with one of the students from the Training School and his wife. He is on his practice year from the school. What dedication and enthusiasm for their work! . . . In one place where there had been only one worker when I began work here six years ago, there were eight workers, all of them ready with ideas and eager to learn. Six of the teachers will go out to banana farms this afternoon and will reach about two hundred children."

With help from a missionary, the people in one town built their own church of cement and wood. It was the first of its kind in the village. When Alice was to hold a vacation Bible school there, she was given a bedroom on the second floor of a private home. When she opened the window on the hot summer night, the neighbors shouted that tigers would jump into her room if she didn't close the window. Directly across the river from the house was the pig-pen where a light was kept burning all night to keep the "tigers" from killing the pigs. Although these "tigers" were really wildcats, they were dangerous, and it was well to take the advice of experience.

In another letter Alice wrote, "a young man who had been a collector on a public bus until he came to the training school was one of the first students to enroll. He had never even taught a Sunday School, and I wondered why he was even accepted to train for the ministry. He almost flunked out the first semester, but he was sincere and kept trying. He fell in love with the girl who had worked for me at the Rural Center. She was bright and had had some experience in church work. In spite of general disapproval of their marriage, they were happy as larks and eventually took over the church. When they first went to their appointment, they had no place to stay and slept on the floor of an old vacant house. There was no organized Sunday School or church, but he spread a sheet over a pile of suitcases for a pulpit. People who came sat on the floor, the bed, stools, or any spot they could find. Neighbors threw rocks on the roof and jeered; but later, when they came asking this young couple to give inoculations, they were obliged. They eventually became friends. When those in the growing services prayed for the sick neighbors, everyone was astonished. Now they came to Sunday School. More than seventy attended an evening service when I was there.

"This young couple didn't know anything about carpentry, but they had to do something to make their home more suitable for church meetings. They tore out a wall and moved another and soon had a good-sized room. A good carpenter helped them put in a skylight, electricity, a shower, and a cement walk. They painted the outside and now have a lovely church with their home on one side."

The Alajuela Training School had no accommodations for couples, but makeshift rooms were finally located so they could continue with their third year of study.

Alice was often called upon to counsel students at the Training School: girls with typical questions about dating, and students who were struggling with difficulties in their interpersonal relationships. Sometimes it seemed that solving these problems was almost as important for their future effectiveness as much of the learning in their classes.

18
Endless Line of Splendor

Helen Hoyt, though never appointed as a salaried missionary, had been invaluable to the mission. She devoted time and energy to the work in the Alajuela church, and her cozy little home became a gathering place for students from the Training School and visitors from other countries.

But Helen passed her eightieth birthday, and her health began to fail. Alice was increasingly concerned about the limitations of living in a foreign country. They made a trip to California and visited several retirement homes. Kingsley Manor in Los Angeles was among the most attractive.

Alice's retirement was fast approaching. Costa Rican workers were demanding more and more autonomy. She was finding that the same desire to take over responsibilities for their own work was emerging in this little Central American republic as in China, halfway around the world. In fact, Alice had worked to encourage it and to prepare for its success.

She left Costa Rica to be with Helen and they took up residence in Kingsley Manor. Helen's health continued to fail, and she lived only three years after their arrival in Los Angeles.

Alice had not yet reached the mandatory retirement age. Since she was an ordained Methodist minister, she asked for an appointment to a Spanish-speaking congregation in southern California. But here in her own native land she met prejudice, even hostility, toward women in the clergy profession. The bishop reluctantly wrote to Costa Rica and learned that she had full clergy rights there. After three years of vague excuses, the Conference finally admitted her to full membership. She was the first woman to achieve such status in the Southern California-Arizona Conference.

She was appointed on a part-time basis, soon working full-time, to a small Spanish-speaking congregation in the tumultous eastern area of Los Angeles. News of riots, robberies, even murder, was speading consternation and alarm across the country.

As she walked the streets of her new parish, she became acquainted with a community where evidences of alcoholism, prostitution, and muggings were all about her. The atmosphere of her little church was upset by a gamut of difficulties, from destructive children running through the property to murders across the street.

There was no church organization. A small group of people merely showed up on Sunday to listen to a program. Alice set about to organize a women's society, a Sunday School, and a day care center. She encouraged self-support; but just as the budget approached the minimum salary set by the Conference, it would be raised because of inflation.

After six years, Alice reached retirement age. The church had become the center of a wide variety of activities and constructive programs. The people in the community were learning to shoulder responsibility for meeting their own needs. Illegal immigrants were not statistics, but real people with problems calling for solutions, if they were to survive in an alien society they had envisioned as the end of the rainbow when they had left their own countries. They were given legal help to move up from abject poverty where they were unable to help themselves. Residents had to be taught to make their voices heard on the political and economic issues of the community. They were taught English as a second language and how to organize for group action. They worked for such improvements as a corner street light where children crossed to go to school. Jobs were found for young people in summer vacation time. Volunteers were organized to help the elderly with their yards and cleaning. Attempts were made to combat crime and drug use. A day care center reached parents as well as children of working mothers. A community developer organized a board joining several churches in the effort to use available community resources.

Alice had never asked for an easy task, and it had never been hers. Even though unable to work in a foreign country as she had dreamed from girlhood, she found opportunity for significant service wherever she happened to be.

One day she was rushed to the hospital. Later she described what happened.

"For some time during the year, I had some trouble that didn't seem to have a name. Finally the doctor put me in the hospital in July for tests. During one of them my heart stopped. During this time I had an experience that impressed me greatly. I suddenly seemed to be looking down on a group of people surrounded by light. They were in an attitude of prayer and I thought, 'I knew people were praying for me, but there are so many!' I had no pain and didn't seem to be concerned with any danger to my life. I was just filled with a confidence that everything was under control. Then the scene faded and I seemed to be struggling with some force too great for me to handle. I didn't know where I was or how I got there. My chest hurt unbearably and I couldn't speak. Gradually I realized that my hand was touching something greasy on my chest and I opened one eye to see the x-ray machine over me. I realized that I was on the operating table and the doctor was saying, 'You are all right now. Cough! Cough!' Burns from the electric shock and sore ribs from attempts to revive me were nothing in comparison with the realization that I was all right.

"My good roommate, Ruth Potter, and her faithful seeing-eye dog, stayed with me like a full-time nurse. Finally, a year later, the doctor put me in the hospital again and I was given a heart pacer. All went well and I have been given the assurance that my heart will behave normally from now on.

"A number of events I wanted to attend had to be missed, but in their place I have learned again the value of prayer and love given generously. It is just as important to learn to receive as to learn to give. It is good to realize that the world can go on without one, but it is impossible to get along without the help of others who act in love."

The world was changing with dizzy rapidity. The early pioneer missionary had spent weeks on the open seas in frail craft to reach his post. Now luxurious jet airplanes covered the same distance in a matter of hours. In place of early physical hardships new problems of administration and personnel were emerging.

Alice Weed's life crossed through this transition. She had known physical hardships and dangers; then had encountered the thrust for independence.

"This one thing I do," wrote St. Paul. Alice's busy creative life has had a single purpose. With total dedication it has led her to make a lasting contribution to the help so needed in this troubled world.

She wrote, "Each person living has a story to tell of the victories over difficulty and evil. Each has a lesson learned that speaks to all mankind of the power implanted in human people for good. Not one life has been lived in vain. If this story of a life lived for a purpose can help someone realize the value of meeting obstacles, conquering defeats and discouragement, then it is worth writing. No matter where one lives there is adventure, the call to sacrifice for good, the opportunity to overcome evil in the power that God gives His children on this earth. When people answer a God-given call, there is nothing physical or spiritual that can stop that purpose from being fulfilled. It may not be where or how it has been envisioned, but it will be fulfilled. Humans cannot destroy the overall purpose that God has in creating the world and his children in it."

"Being confident in this very thing, that he which hath begun a good work in you will perform it until the day of Jesus Christ." (Philippians 1:6)

19
China Thirty-two Years Later

It was October, 1982.

A Japanese jetliner circled over the city of Peking and dropped to a smooth landing beside the large, modern airport.

Among deplaning passengers, an American with softly curling gray hair and eyes sparkling with anticipation made her way among other western-clad travelers scattered thinly through the new airport built for future throngs. There was nothing in the vast, high-ceilinged building to remind Alice Weed of the dockside din and confusion which had greeted her on her first arrival in Shanghai by ocean liner years before.

At the exit she stopped to look about her. Could this be China, the country she had been forced to leave so ruthlessly in 1950? No coolies stood beside picturesque rickshaws shouting invitations to accept their transportation. Only buses and occasional automobiles came and went impersonally. This was a country unbelievably different from the land where she had begun her missionary work, work in a foreign land to which she had dedicated her life.

The trip from Peking to Chengtu by airplane offered not the slightest resemblance to her hazardous journey through Indo-China and up the

Burma Road forty-two years before. When she reached Chengtu, Alice found it changed beyond recognition. Public buildings and highrise houses reached to the sky, often from clusters of raw, new construction. In most places trees lined wide boulevards. Buses, government automobiles and trucks rode through the streets with blaring horns. Wide lanes on either side of many streets thronged with busy people on foot and on bicycles.

Individual distinctions blurred in the working clothes uniformly worn by men and women: loose-fitting, blue, baggy pants, and formless jackets. Chinese love of color found expression in children's gaily colored clothes. Occasionally, a passerby grinned and tried out a newly learned English phrase on Alice as she made her way through the swarms of people.

Alice was eager to visit old familiar places where she had worked during those difficult years. But the Methodist church was gone. It had been burned during the Cultural Revolution. The house where she had lived was now an office building, the last of the cluster of buildings where a group of missionaries had lived and worked.

Homes, Alice learned, were plain, sparsely furnished and seriously overcrowded. Some of the occupants were disappointed but resigned. All of them had learned to live with severe limitations and inconveniences.

On Sunday, Alice went to church with others of her tour group. It was crowded beyond capacity with Christian worshipers. Denominational lines were lost as all came together as one big family. The government prohibited — and the church refused — any sort of control from a foreign country, demanding that the Chinese provide their own leadership without foreign "interference." Each individual was allowed to worship as he chose. Religion was not encouraged, but some leaders believed that it "was good for" the people. But it must be without risk of any foreign influence through workers from other countries. Bibles were printed by the government and were made available through the churches.

Many Christians were still uneasy, unsure of safety from the persecutions of the past. They took part in church life with caution.

In the Sunday morning congregation, Alice found fourteen people she had known when she had worked there. Some had suffered abuse, even prison, and others persecution; but they did not talk about it. They were living now, they said, and the trials and tribulations of the past were to be forgotten as they looked forward to a better future.

Later, when Alice returned to the States, a friend said, "You worked so hard and experienced such difficulties in China, and now there seems to be so little left to show for it. Truthfully, was it all worthwhile?"

"Oh *yes!*" was Alice's immediate reply. "Governments, economic developments and lifestyles may come and go. Leadership, worship forms, even physical settings, vary inevitably. But the need of human beings for the vitalizing force of Christian love never changes. The physical evidence of a missionary's work may not remain, but the Christian spirit carries on. Taking the message of Christ's love to needy people wherever they may be in this troubled world has been my single life's purpose."

With St. Paul she might have said, "THIS ONE THING I DO."